AN INVESTORS PRESS GUIDE FOR
401(k) ADMINISTRATORS

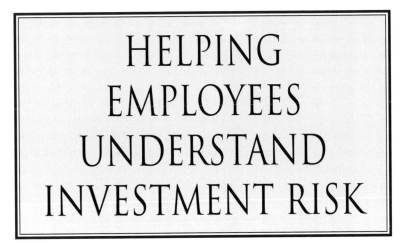

HELPING
EMPLOYEES
UNDERSTAND
INVESTMENT RISK

A PRIMER FOR MAKING ASSET
ALLOCATION DECISIONS

INVESTORS
PRESS

Copyright © 1996 by Investors Press, Inc.
World rights reserved. No part of this publication may be stored in a retrieval system, transmitted or reproduced in any way, including but not limited to photocopy, photograph, magnetic or other record, without the prior agreement and written permission of the Publisher. Making more than one (1) copy, and for other than strictly personal use, is absolutely prohibited. Bulk copies of this publication may be obtained as explained on the order page at the back of the book.

All rights reserved under International and Pan-American Copyright Conventions.

Published in the United States by Investors Press, Inc.

Library of Congress Cataloging-in-Publication Data
        Investors Press, Inc.
        Helping Employees Understand Investment Risk:
        A Primer for Making Asset Allocation Decisions
            ISBN 1-885123-06-X

Printed in Mexico

10 9   8   7   6   5   4   3   2   1

Jacket art and design © by Wendell Minor
Book and chart design by Silver Communications Inc.
Mid-Range Editon

ACKNOWLEDGEMENT

Helping Employees Understand Investment Risk: A Primer for Making Asset Allocation Decisions is the second Investors Press Guide for 401(k) Plan Administrators. Each Guide in this special Defined Contribution Series examines issues of compelling concern to those responsible for managing and administering their organization's 401(k) plans. A compendium of leading-edge 401(k) thinking, each book in the Series is an easy-to-use, practical guide and an informative, continuing reference resource.

Investors Press acknowledges with appreciation the immeasurable help and cooperation it received in the research and preparation of **Helping Employees Understand Investment Risk.** Special thanks go to the following plan sponsors, consultants, education providers and industry and government leaders whose generosity in sharing their ideas, insights and analyses contributed to the value of this book as a primer to help employees make more informed asset allocation decisions.

ADVANCED MICRO DEVICES
AEROSPACE
ASEA BROWN BOVERI, INC.
BECHTEL CORPORATION
CONSECO
DAYTON HUDSON CORPORATION
DIGITAL EQUIPMENT CORPORATION
ELI LILLY & CO.
HALLIBURTON COMPANY
IBM CORPORATION
THE KROGER CO.
MOBIL CORPORATION
MONTANA POWER COMPANY
NAVISTAR
NESTLE USA, INC.

PEPSICO
PUBLIC SERVICE ELECTRIC & GAS
TEXAS UTILITIES COMPANY
THE TIMES MIRROR COMPANY
U S WEST
XEROX

ACCESS RESEARCH, INC.
THE ALBIN COMPANIES OF OHIO
ARNERICH MASSENA EDUCATION
THE AYCO COMPANY
DISCOVER LEARNING, INC.
EMPLOYEE BENEFIT RESEARCH
  INSTITUTE (EBRI)
HEWITT ASSOCIATES
401(K) VENTURES

Helping Employees Understand Investment Risk: A Primer for Making Asset Allocation Decisions is underwritten by a distinguished group of providers from across the country to whom special appreciation goes from everyone who values the importance of education and the candid exchange of information. Their commitment makes this Guide available to you—the men and women who are charged with meeting the increasingly complex daily challenges of helping your employees understand investment risk in order to achieve retirement security.

INVESTORS
PRESS

Underwritten by

ALLMERICA FINANCIAL INSTITUTIONAL SERVICES

AMERICAN EXPRESS FINANCIAL ADVISORS INC.

CIGNA RETIREMENT & INVESTMENT SERVICES

DIVERSIFIED INVESTMENT ADVISORS

FIDELITY INVESTMENTS®

FLEET INVESTMENT ADVISORS

METLIFE

NATIONSBANK

NEUBERGER & BERMAN MANAGEMENT INC.

NYL BENEFIT SERVICES COMPANY, INC.

PRUDENTIAL DEFINED CONTRIBUTION SERVICES (PRU-DC)

ROGERS, CASEY & ASSOCIATES, INC.

STANWICH BENEFITS GROUP, INC.

STRONG FUNDS

T. ROWE PRICE ASSOCIATES, INC.

TABLE OF CONTENTS

INTRODUCTION

The 401(k) plan is the quintessential 1990s investment account — a benefit that epitomizes the transition from corporate paternalism to employee self-reliance. For many Americans under fifty, this self-directed defined contribution pension will be their biggest single retirement asset. For some employees, it will be the only retirement asset they accumulate other than Social Security. Its ultimate value will depend on the decisions employees make themselves — and the success of those decisions will depend in large part on their understanding of investment risk.

This fundamental shift in financial responsibility for retirement security presents employers with an unprecedented challenge. As benefits providers, their traditional role has been to protect their employees from risk, not teach them how to accept and manage it. Now many employers are beginning to realize that, as 401(k) plan sponsors, they have assumed a new and different responsibility: the obligation to provide their employees with the investment education and range of investment choices they need to succeed as their own pension fund managers.

Most employers are still struggling to define the extent of their new corporate responsibility. Designing a 401(k) communications plan and investment menu that meet the diverse educational and individual financial needs of growing numbers of plan participants is, indeed, a complex challenge.

For many companies, assuming this new role represents a difficult cultural adjustment. Often, their instinct is to shield employees from potential loss by offering only the most conservative 401(k) investment choices, and to protect the corporation from potential liability by scrupulously avoiding any communication that might be interpreted as investment advice. Ironically, the plan sponsor's caution on both counts exposes plan participants to the gravest long-term danger: the risk of taking too little risk to earn the investment return necessary to fund a comfortable retirement.

Even truly innovative plan sponsors—those companies offering broadly diversified 401(k) investment menus and assuming an unprecedented role as their employees' primary investment educators—are uncertain about how to navigate in such deep and uncharted waters.

WANTED: AN INVESTMENT EDUCATION FOR A NEW BREED OF PENSION FUND MANAGERS

401(k) plans represent the fastest growing pool of pension money in the United States: more than $525 billion of assets, expanding at approximately 15% a year. By the year 2000, this pool of assets will exceed $1 trillion. Responsibility for investing this staggering sum rests with 18.5 million plan participants—a diverse group of inexperienced, risk-averse new pension fund managers who often lack the education and self-confidence to make their own investment decisions.

Most of these novice pension fund managers do not understand how the investment market works; many aren't sure what a stock or a bond or a money market fund is or how these investments produce financial gains or losses.[1] In most cases, they don't know that different asset classes have very different characteristics and historic returns, or understand that their appropriateness as investments depends in large part on each investor's personal needs and time horizon.

Most important, all too many 401(k) plan participants associate risk entirely with short-term fluctuations in the value of their accounts; they overlook the critical long-term danger that inflation will devour the returns they earn in stable, low-risk investments.

Equally troubling is the fact that very few 401(k) investors have a specific dollars and cents investment goal for their retirement accounts. According to a 1994 national survey by Public Agenda, seven in ten Americans don't know how much money they'll need in retirement, and 37% substantially underestimate the percentage of their current yearly income they'll need to maintain their standard of living—the lifestyle a majority say they want and expect in retirement.[2]

Because most plan participants are painfully aware that they don't possess the knowledge or information necessary to make sound investment decisions, their main goal is to avoid any risk of losing their principal, rather than to assume reasonable risks to make it grow. Rather than wander in confusion among investments that appear equally bewildering to them, they stick with what they think they understand: an interest-bearing account like a Guaranteed Investment Contract or a money market fund, or a bond fund they mistakenly assume is no riskier than an interest-bearing account.

Paradoxically, the typical result is an asset allocation that professional pension fund managers would reject unhesitatingly as both naive and risky: the predominant share of employee-directed 401(k) assets is in low-growth stable value funds.[3]

---

[1] A 1994 national survey of 1,000 working Americans by benefits consultant Towers Perrin found that 39% of those surveyed didn't know how their money was allocated among the asset classes. Of those who did know, 33% said they had no money invested in stocks; 32% believed there is no risk at all associated with an investment in bonds; and 14% believed there is no risk at all to investments in a balanced fund.

[2] Public Agenda, based in New York City, conducted a 35-minute telephone survey of 1,100 randomly drawn members of the general public in August 1994. The survey was restricted to non-retired individuals between the ages of 22 and 61.

[3] Access Research, Inc. estimates that as of year-end 1994, 32% of 401(k) plan assets was invested in Guaranteed Investment Contracts or money market funds, 23% was invested in company stock and 19% was invested in equity funds. The balance was invested in fixed-income and balanced funds.

To the extent that employees do invest retirement money in equities, too often it's concentrated in the stock of a single company—their own employer.[4]

Employee over-reliance on company stock can limit the employers' flexibility, as well. "If a company has 50% of its defined contribution plan assets invested in its own stock and the stock loses 50% of its value over three years, what happens to the employees who want to retire during that time?" asks Donald Sauvigne, Director of Retirement and Capital Accumulations Programs at IBM. "These employees can't retire and the company can't replenish its workforce."

AN UNSATISFACTORY STATUS QUO

This investment status quo is fraught with risk and frustration for plan sponsors and participants alike.

Nothing is more baffling to human resource managers than low employee participation in a 401(k) plan they have carefully designed to feature a varied menu of investment choices and a generous company match. But employees who don't understand the relative risks and rewards of their investment choices typically save very little or don't participate in the 401(k) plan at all. This creates a risk for the plan itself: the danger that it will flunk Federal non-discrimination tests because the company's highly paid employees are saving a substantially greater percentage of their salary than are lower-paid employees.[5]

Employees who have no framework in which to assess the likelihood of investment loss are understandably—indeed, sensibly—reluctant to risk their money. Education can provide that framework, explain the potential risks and rewards in each type of investment, and use historical rates of return and volatility to show employees what they can reasonably expect from each investment choice.

---

[4] The amount of employer stock in defined contribution plans nearly tripled during the 1980s. The Employee Retirement Income Security Act (ERISA) prohibits defined benefit plans from investing more than 10% of plan assets in employer stock; no such limitation exists for 401(k) plans. A 1995 analysis of Labor Department data by Rutgers University School of Management and Labor Relations shows that as of year-end 1991, the most recent year with complete data available, an average of 17% of assets in defined contribution plans were invested in employer stock. A 1994 study of 401(k) plans at 1,034 companies by benefits consultant Hewitt Associates found that 30 of the respondents had their own stock as their only 401(k) investment option.

From the employee's perspective, concentrating 401(k) assets in employer stock epitomizes the danger of non-diversification: if the company encounters financial difficulties, the employee can lose his or her paycheck and nest egg at the same time.

[5] 29% of the 900 plan sponsors surveyed by benefits consultant Foster Higgins in 1994 had to make adjustments to pass the Actual Deferral Percentage (ADP) test. The vast majority (78%) did so by limiting the amount of their highly compensated employees' pre-tax contributions. 7% of the plan sponsors surveyed passed the test by re-characterizing pre-tax contributions as after-tax contributions, thereby increasing the taxable income of the highly compensated plan participants. Foster Higgins asked plan sponsors who didn't need to make adjustments to pass the tests if they had taken action during the year to improve their test results. Nearly one-fifth of the respondents (18%) said they had added to or changed employee communication—often after analyzing the demographics of non-participants.

WHEN BEST INTENTIONS AREN'T ENOUGH

Material distributed to 401(k) plan participants frequently falls far short of providing such a framework. Many participants receive little more than a bare bones explanation of plan mechanics and a few sketchy generalities about investing—perhaps only a blanket statement that the fixed-income fund is a more conservative investment and the stock fund is more aggressive.

Those few employers who try to communicate more useful information often discover that explaining investment risk in language non-professional investors can understand is a greater challenge than they anticipated. An educational brochure that passes muster with corporate, legal and financial staff, for example, is often incomprehensible to employees who have no investing experience or knowledge of financial markets. A pamphlet that explains basic investment concepts using terms like "risk/return characteristics" and "standard deviation" may seem like elementary education to a corporate pension fund manager, but such unfamiliar language merely reinforces the average employee's presumption that investing is an arcane discipline beyond his or her grasp.

Despite the best intentions and significant investments of time and money, educational efforts frequently fail because they overestimate employees' knowledge. Diversification, for example, is a basic concept that professionals take for granted, but it's often a new one to people who don't manage investments for a living.

DANGERS AHEAD

Plan sponsors have both self-serving and altruistic reasons to allay their employees' fears and insecurities about investing and explain the dangers they court by taking too little investment risk. The potential long-term consequences of low 401(k) participation and insufficient investment returns are clear: a generation of older employees who can't afford to retire would damage the plan sponsor's reputation and make it difficult to attract and retain ambitious younger employees.

Legal liabilities cloud the horizon as well. Employees who haven't saved or invested well enough to retire comfortably may sue their former employers, alleging they weren't warned of the dangers of investing too conservatively, failing to diversify or trying to time the market.

Growing concern about this potential corporate liability has spurred an increasing number of legal departments to reexamine their long-standing reluctance to offer employees material that might be interpreted as investment advice. Increasingly, employers try to distinguish the difference between investment advice and investment education. The new interest in offering investment education has also been fueled by the Department of Labor's 404(c) regulation, which limits employer liability for employee-directed investments when the employer offers at least three distinct investment choices, gives an adequate explanation of these choices and allows participants to transfer money between them with sufficient frequency.

Corporate interest in educating employees about risk has been heightened, too, by the 401(k) plan's growing visibility as a retirement benefit. For many companies these plans are no longer a supplemental benefit, but the primary pension plan. And the market has responded: 401(k) product and service providers, eager to differentiate themselves from their competitors, offer more and more generic employee education and communication programs that can be customized to fit any plan sponsor's requirements, often for no charge or for only nominal fees. Today, an impressive variety of investment education programs is readily available to employers of every size.

A FIELD IN ITS INFANCY

Despite the wide availability of 401(k) educational programs, this field is still in its infancy. Many so-called educational programs are little more than packages of promotional materials from the providers who offer them. Many of these programs are equal parts marketing and generic information. Even the best education packages are still evolving through ongoing research by plan providers and plan sponsors.

Adult education has never been undertaken on such an ambitious scale before and plan sponsors are increasingly aware that successful educational programs must be part of an ongoing process that requires constant reevaluation and fine-tuning. Employers seriously committed to employee education know that it takes more than one 45-minute session to help employees achieve long-term financial self-reliance as informed and confident investors. Mounting evidence strongly suggests that ongoing investment education programs both increase plan participants' willingness to take prudent investment risk and help raise overall plan participation.[6]

MEETING THE NEEDS OF TWO AUDIENCES

Any sound investment education program has to explain basic concepts like the importance of asset allocation, diversification, the magic of compounding and the investor's time horizon, as well as provide essential "nuts and bolts" information, including the history of stock versus bond performance.

But human beings aren't as easy to program as computers. In real life, no one learns to invest in the abstract. Plan sponsors often find that investment concepts and plan features don't really start to make sense to employees until they are personalized with questions about their family, needs and goals. In other words, education really begins when the individual gets a personal financial planning focus.

This personal finance focus is especially important to the many employees who really don't want to learn the intricacies of investing. Although these people feel a strong sense of responsibility to make good financial decisions for their families, they have no interest in learning about investing—and experience has taught that adults only learn what they want to learn.

---

[6] The 1994 survey of 900 plan sponsors by benefits consultant Foster Higgins found that plan participation rose in 64% of the plans that increased their communications programs. Also, numerous plan sponsors have found that investment education encourages participants to increase their contributions to equity funds and reduce their contributions to stable value and money market funds. At IBM, for example, Don Sauvigne, Director of Retirement and Capital Accumulation Programs, considers continuing education partly responsible for the fact that employee contributions to fixed-income investments in the IBM plan fell from 65% to 45% of all employee-directed contributions between 1993 and 1995.

There may be a dozen different demographic groups in any one company, but all employees fall into one of two basic categories: *those who want to learn how to actively manage their retirement investments and those who don't*. Provider research has found that these two fundamentally different groups exist in very kind of company: the difference doesn't reflect the employee's age, income or education, but rather, his or her personal interest and motivation.

Many employees who aren't interested in learning how to manage their money go out of their way to avoid the subject. To reach them, an educational campaign needs light touches and appealingly simple materials—balloons, unintimidating connect-the-dots games, cartoon characters, the testimonials of known and trusted colleagues who already participate in the plan. They need a program that says clearly: "This is for you, not for the financial nerd who's good at it." Providers and plan sponsors have found that these user-friendly touches don't turn off the employees who are truly interested in investment education. People who want to learn about investing like talking about financial issues so much they aren't easily bored; but to satisfy them, the program must also address substantive questions in greater depth.

Employees who aren't interested in investing typically save too little and over-value stability of principal. When they talk about stocks, they often use words like "gamble" and "take a chance." Many providers and plan sponsors have found that these participants prefer pre-mixed investments, such as the increasingly popular lifecycle funds. They respond to the idea of hiring a portfolio manager to do asset allocation for them.

Those employees who want to actively manage their retirement investments often focus excessively on return, take market-timing risks and change investments on a piecemeal basis, often without creating long-term strategies for their portfolios. These eager investors read the personal finance columns and chase hot ideas. They're motivated to become experts themselves and do their own asset allocation. Often, they want a longer menu of investment choices.

Some plan sponsors find that a two-tiered communications approach is the best way to reach both employee groups. Xerox set an example in 1994 when it produced a two-brochure communications package for its 401(k) participants and enrollees in conjunction with the introduction of three new equity fund investment options.

The first brochure explained basic investment concepts and gave a brief description of the advantages and disadvantages of each available fund, with graphs illustrating risk and return. The second brochure had a much more detailed description of each fund and was targeted to employees who want to learn more. The company included a survey form in its double communication package asking employees to rate its helpfulness. Response was overwhelmingly favorable—and the communications package seems to have increased employees' comfort level with investment risk. "We have seen employees shift money out of the lower risk funds and into the higher risk funds," says Myra Drucker, Assistant Treasurer.

The New Order: Paternalism Redefined

The transition from traditional corporate paternalism to employee self-reliance is difficult for both employers and employees. Many mid-sized or small manufacturing and retail firms have no tradition of communicating with their employees and lack the kind of infrastructure that makes communication easy. Understandably, teaching people on loading docks and factory floors seems a daunting task.

But for most of corporate America, traditional paternalism is simply no longer affordable. The 401(k) plan is immensely popular with both employers and employees and is clearly here to stay. Increasingly, employers believe that part of their charge as 401(k) fiduciaries is to see that their employees understand the plan and are comfortable enough with investment risk to use it to their own best advantage. Now that employees are responsible for their own financial futures, the "new" paternalism helps them help themselves by teaching them how to manage investment risk well enough to make informed investment decisions.

The only effective way to build employees' confidence in their ability to make sound investment decisions is to expand their understanding of risk and increase their ability to manage it. Today, the most innovative companies continue to push the boundaries of adult education, searching for ways to empower their employees as they meet the challenge and responsibility of managing their own retirement assets.

Lynn Brenner

CHAPTER
ONE

The Psychologies of Risk

Lynn Brenner

As all professional investors know, risk is a two-sided coin: potential capital growth is the flip side of possible capital loss. That makes risk acceptable, even desirable, to investors because their goal is to grow their money. In fact, for an investor, *the biggest risk is taking no risk at all.* Without risk, there's no opportunity for growth.

But most 401(k) participants don't think of themselves as investors. They see themselves simply as savers—and savers have a very different perspective because they have a very different goal: their objective is to avoid losing their money and their view of risk is almost entirely negative.

Changing this entrenched "saver's perspective" is investment education's most compelling goal. A successful educational program can teach participants and eligible enrollees to think of themselves as competent investors who can use their 401(k) plans as long-term investment vehicles. It does this by dispelling the three most common participant misconceptions:

1. "Investing requires specialized knowledge that I don't have and that takes years to acquire."
2. "Investing is just another form of gambling and I'm not a gambler."
3. "I don't need to know anything about investing because I save money and that's all that matters."

The Psychology of Risk Aversion: "Better Safe Than Sorry"

When savers put $1,000 into a Certificate of Deposit, they know they'll get their $1,000 back plus interest. They're comfortable knowing their $1,000 won't grow to $2,000 or shrink to $500 because their main concern is to be sure their money is there when they need it. Many employees have exactly the same concern when it comes to their 401(k) accounts. They're afraid that if they take risks with their retirement money, it won't be there when they need it. Their biggest fear is losing principal.

Some employees are convinced that "safe" investments earn more than "risky" ones over the long run. When Towers Perrin surveyed 1,000 working Americans in 1994, 35% of the respondents said guaranteed investments would produce higher returns than stocks over a 20-year period and 15% said guaranteed investments would perform as well as stocks.[1]

Employees still prefer safety, even when they realize greater risk means a higher potential return. Fifty percent of the Towers Perrin respondents said the most important factor in investing their money is a guaranteed return, as opposed to the potential for a higher return that involves some risk. In a nutshell, their view is, "Even if I make less money in guaranteed investments, at least I won't lose any. It's better to be safe than sorry."

What these employees don't understand, of course, is that in the long-run they *will* lose in guaranteed investments because they'll lose the battle against inflation: they won't earn enough to finance the comfortable retirement they want and expect. "I tell people that anything guaranteed not to decline in value is also guaranteed to lose ground to inflation and if you don't beat inflation, you're never going to accumulate enough money to retire," says Jonathan Pond, financial planner and author,[2] who also conducts 401(k) educational seminars.

Service providers, financial planners and the media have been repeating this same message for years. Warnings about the dangers of not keeping ahead of inflation haven't fallen on entirely deaf ears: there is evidence that plan participants today are somewhat more willing to take investment risk with their new contributions.

A 1994 Access Research, Inc., (ARI) survey of U.S. households found the overall split of current 401(k) plan contributions was 70% equity and 30% fixed-income. But ARI found that only 19% of existing 401(k) balances are invested in equities, excluding company stock. "People are almost twice as likely to change the allocation of money they're depositing as they are to move their previously deposited assets," says Gerald O'Connor, ARI's Director of Research.[3]

---

[1] Benefits consultant Towers Perrin conducted a telephone survey of 1,000 working Americans in 1994. Households were randomly selected, but the survey was restricted to those working for organizations with at least 1,000 employees. Of survey respondents, 52% were men, 48% were women and 58% were married. 35% of respondents had household income under $35,000; 24% had household income between $35,000 and $50,000 and 35% had household income over $50,000.

[2] **The New Century Family Money Book,** New York: Doubleday, 1994.

[3] Access Research, Inc., a research-based market planning and communications company, mailed an 8-page survey to 10,000 randomly selected U.S. households in September 1994. 1,317 completed questionnaires from 401(k) participants and 23 completed questionnaires from Salary Reduction Simplified Employee Pension (SARSEP) participants were received in October 1994 and tabulated for cluster analysis, a technique that groups respondents in clusters based on similar patterns of answers. The survey was restricted to male and female heads of household, employed full-time and with household income over $20,000. Slightly more than half the respondents worked for companies with 1,000 employees or more; 38% worked for companies with fewer than 500 employees.

An Investing Profile for Every Participant Personality

Although risk aversion is clearly common among inexperienced investors, any group of 401(k) plan participants includes a broad range of attitudes, concerns and misconceptions about financial options and investment strategies. Plan sponsors must be aware of them as they structure their educational efforts. According to Kathleen Gurney, Chairman of Financial Psychology Corporation and creator of the Moneymax Profiling System, there are nine distinct "money personalities."[4]

Gurney's extensive research found that although some of these "personalities" show marginal overlapping and share some characteristics, each is distinct enough to be classified as a separate group. She describes the following groups, which she discovered are evenly distributed in the population as a whole:

- **Safety Players:** Often well-educated, they nevertheless lack the confidence to take investment risk. Fear of loss overwhelms them and they often perceive an inordinate amount of risk in vehicles that aren't that risky. They feel they can't take control of their finances and rationalize their behavior with reasons why they shouldn't try. For example, they might say: "Even if I study this, I can't have any control. How can I know what to do? Even people on Wall Street don't always make the right decision."

- **Entrepreneurs:** They enjoy the power and prestige that money brings, reward themselves for working by buying the best cars, houses and wines and are very comfortable with stock market risk. Their blind spot is that they feel they can do anything. Their yearning for personal challenge leads them to take on too much risk.

- **Optimists:** They're more interested in day-to-day "personal happiness" than in worrying about making their money grow for some distant tomorrow. Optimists are laid-back; detached from their financial affairs, they avoid any stress that could shadow their enjoyment of life. Their attitude is "Money isn't all that important to me. Somehow, the future will take care of itself."

- **Hunters:** Highly educated, often well-paid and professionally successful, they have a live-for-today approach to finance. They spend impulsively to reward themselves for working so hard and postpone saving for another day.

- **Achievers:** Well-educated, hard-working, proud of their accomplishments, they tend to distrust others with their money. Achievers are take-charge types with a strong need to control their own money. They're conservative investors; they don't want to risk assets they worked hard to accumulate.

- **Perfectionists:** They, too, don't trust other people with their money, but they don't trust themselves either. Perfectionists are so afraid of making a mistake, they avoid making a decision. They perceive high risk in practically every investment.

---

[4] The Moneymax R© is a tool that helps defined contribution plan participants understand their money management styles and needs. It puts that knowledge to work in helping them make decisions about their investment opportunities. Kathleen Gurney, a psychologist, developed her theory of nine money personalities in 1981. It has since been tested in surveys of more than 30,000 individuals by statisticians at six national market research firms.

RISK: YOU CAN'T LIVE WITH IT, YOU CAN'T LIVE WITHOUT IT.

 *It's an inescapable fact of life. But one that is seldom grasped by 401(k) plan participants. They fear risk in part because they understand it only in the narrow context of losing their money.*  *They need to understand that risk can be managed, and that without it, many will have no chance of achieving a financially secure retirement.*  *At T. Rowe Price, we look at investing as a marathon, not a sprint. Our goal is to help employees manage risk by providing them with investment options that can help them achieve long-term financial security. Many of our funds have earned Morningstar's best ratings for risk-adjusted performance. Our asset allocation funds help investors reduce risk while providing the potential to achieve attractive returns.*  *It's only natural to be concerned about risk. But with the right investment firm, maybe your employees will start to think of risk not as a problem, but as an opportunity.*  *If you'd like to learn about how we can help your employees become more confident investors, please call John R. Rockwell at (410) 581-5900.*

Invest With Confidence®
T. Rowe Price

There are many reasons why employees choose not to participate in a 401(k) plan. Some employees don't join because they are risk-averse or lack the self-confidence they need to make their own investment decisions. More often, however, failure to join the plan reflects employees' conviction that they have too little disposable income to put money away for what seems a very distant future.

Indeed, plan sponsor communications strategies must grapple with the reality that few Americans make it a priority to save for retirement; not surprisingly, they tend to focus on day-to-day problems and expenses. A 1994 Public Agenda Foundation study found that 73% of its 1,100 non-retired respondents thought they *should* put aside more money for retirement, but said they were overwhelmed by more immediate demands on their money.[8] As one respondent put it, "Between the day-care and the mortgage and the car payments, we're *trying* to save—but really, we're just taking care of today."

Even a few key plan features can motivate these non-savers to participate. Public Agenda found that 8 out of 10 respondents felt that automatic payroll deduction was the best way for them to save for retirement, and of those who had the hardest time saving, most liked the idea of a vehicle that keeps retirement money out of their reach.

The Public Agenda focus groups also suggested that there are times when non-participants are particularly responsive to the plan sponsor's pitch to join the 401(k) plan:

➤ when they get a raise

➤ on their major birthdays: 30, 40, and 50

➤ when their children leave home

➤ when their own parents retire

INVESTMENT EDUCATION BASICS: A FIVE-STEP PROCESS

Most experts agree that despite varying participant personalities, there is a five-step process that helps employees develop or increase their comfort level with investment risk, while it enhances their ability to make decisions appropriate to their financial needs and risk tolerance.

A good educational program must:

1. Explain the basics—in a very basic way.

Plan participant investment education should begin with a nuts and bolts explanation of what stocks, bonds and money market instruments are and how—based on their historical performance—they can be expected to behave over different time

---

[8] The Public Agenda survey was done in cooperation with EBRI, the Washington, DC-based Employee Benefit Research Institute. Both are non-profit, non-partisan organizations. Public Agenda conducted 16 focus groups with approximately 160 people in 1993 and 1994 in Atlanta, Boston, Chicago, Cincinnati, Denver, Fort Lee, San Antonio and San Diego. Overall, the groups represented a demographic cross-section of the general population. Two focus groups were held in each city. Public Agenda also conducted a 35-minute telephone survey of 1,100 randomly drawn members of the general public in August 1994. The telephone survey was restricted to non-retired individuals between the ages of 22 and 61.

RIGHT NOW SOMEONE IN YOUR COMPANY WHO DOESN'T KNOW THE DIFFERENCE BETWEEN A STOCK AND A BOND IS DECIDING HOW TO INVEST THEIR 401*K* MONEY.

Perhaps you've seen that blank stare in an employee's eyes as you try to explain their investment options. Getting people to really understand is a challenge. One that T. Rowe Price has been meeting ever since 401(k) plans came into existence. We realize that the more people know about their plan and their investment options, the more likely they are to make sound decisions. That's why T. Rowe Price offers a full range of communications programs—from seminars and videos to newsletters and retirement planning software. We understand that some of your employees are sophisticated investors and others are novices, so we tailor our programs to help people at both ends of the spectrum and everyone in between. In many cases, your employees' future financial security will be riding on how wisely they invest their 401(k) money. The more they know, the better their chances are. If you'd like to learn about how we can help your employees become more confident investors, please call John R. Rockwell at (410) 581-5900.

Invest With Confidence®

T. Rowe Price

T. Rowe Price Investment Services, Inc., Distributor.

horizons. Even knowledgeable employees often find a review of this elementary information reassuring confirmation that their understanding is correct.

Plan sponsors often assume most employees understand more than they actually do, says J. Perry Conley, Deferred Benefits Director at The Kroger Co., especially if the human resource people don't think of themselves as being particularly financially sophisticated. Plan administrators may think " 'Well, I don't know that much about finance and if I know what the S&P 500 is, everybody does.' But the reality is that they don't." After listening to Kroger employee focus groups discussing 401(k) plan investments, Conley concluded that it's almost impossible to underestimate employees' financial knowledge. His favorite illustration of the point:

> "Some stocks are Standard and some are Poor."
> —Plan participant

"We have an S&P 500 Index fund as one of our investment choices and one question we asked focus groups was 'Do you know what the Standard & Poor's 500 is?' In any group, there's always someone trying to impress his or her co-workers. The someone in this group, who'd been right about some things and wrong about others, immediately said he knew what Standard & Poor's stood for. Everyone else was quiet while he explained that every year, some stocks are standard and some are poor."

A simple, understandable recap of the basics often gives employees answers to questions they are too embarrassed to ask. Many people are reluctant to expose their lack of knowledge. The more intelligent, educated and sophisticated they are, in fact, the greater their reluctance to ask "dumb" questions. Plan sponsors and service providers have found one important reason to invite spouses to educational meetings is that they ask questions; very often employees don't because they're afraid to risk looking stupid in front of their peers.

Many employees know they don't understand enough about their investment options to make an intelligent assessment of the risks and rewards involved. Focus groups at Kroger told the company something it hadn't realized before: many participants with low savings rates had never increased their contributions, not because they couldn't afford to, but because they didn't understand the investments.

People who don't understand all their available investment options tend to gravitate to the one they feel they understand best because it seems the least risky, often assuming bigger investment risks than they realize. "I worry when I hear a 62-year-old production worker saying all his 401(k) money is in company stock because it's the safest place to be," says Conley. "Company stock was the only investment option he could understand and therefore he believed it was the safest."

Plan sponsors must explain the danger of concentrating all of one's assets in any single investment. *The importance of reducing risk through diversification* is a basic concept among professional investors, but is unfamiliar to many plan participants. Inexperienced investors frequently assume incorrectly that their most prudent course of action is to concentrate their assets in a single "safe" investment.

Plan sponsors must also explain that thanks to the magic of compounding, participants who save even very small amounts early in life will build a bigger nest egg than those who postpone saving until they can afford to make larger contributions.

2. Explain the different kinds of risk.

Many employees are concerned exclusively with the risk of losing their principal. Others know that isn't the only danger they face, but aren't sure what other risks lie hidden in asset classes they don't fully understand. They need to hear about:

➤ **Inflation Risk:** Few plan participants consider the very real danger that their investment returns may be substantially reduced, or even wiped out, by increases in the cost of living. They should be reminded how much more a loaf of bread costs today than it did ten years ago. If the inflation rate is 3%, a 4% money market return is really worth only 1% in purchasing power—before taxes.

➤ **Market Risk:** Many plan participants fear the value of stocks will fall because of unpredictable market changes. It's important to acknowledge that this is a realistic fear for short-term investors, as well as to point out that market risk is a much less significant danger for long-term investors. Over a ten-year period or longer, individual companies may go broke and entire industries may shrink significantly, but a well-diversified group of U.S. businesses is very likely to weather changes and keep growing—in part by raising the price of goods and services they sell. Their shareholders' investment will grow, too.

➤ **Credit Risk:** Most plan participants understand the risk that a bond issuer may default on principal or interest payments. But often, they mistakenly assume that credit risk is the only potential danger in bond investments, unaware of the danger of interest rate risk.

➤ **Interest Rate Risk:** The danger that a fixed-income investment may shrink in value because of a change in interest rates is probably the least understood investment risk. Many plan participants mistakenly assume that when interest rates go up, their total return from interest-paying investments goes up, too. They do not realize that when interest rates rise, the price of bonds falls. In fact, the Towers Perrin survey found that 32% of respondents believed there was "no risk at all" associated with an investment in bonds!

➤ **Currency Risk:** The danger that changes in foreign exchange rates will reduce the dollar value of overseas investments. This is an important risk to explain in a plan that offers international funds.

3. Encourage realistic expectations.

Nearly every education program stresses the fact that stocks produced a 10.29% average annual return between 1926 and 1994. But charts showing how stock volatility diminishes over time can be misleading, says Larry Elkin, a financial planner and author who has conducted pre-retirement seminars for employees, because they can unintentionally leave the impression that the stock market is a consistently high-performing investment. Employees need to understand that the stock market is an investment that is high-performing in the long-run, but produces highly inconsistent returns over the short-term.

"To manage expectations, you have to sell the instability up-front," Elkin says. "Emphasizing the market's long-term 10% annual return doesn't prepare people for what happens along the way. The statistical probability is that the stock market will average one down year every four years. An investor who knows that's normal will react very differently to a down year than an investor who thinks in terms of a 10% annual return."[9]

Inexperienced investors also need a framework in which to analyze the significance of their losses. It helps them to know that a loss in a growth fund is no cause for alarm when growth funds in general are down. Employees should be encouraged to compare the performance of their investments with appropriate benchmarks and similar investments. New investors sometimes expect that "good" investments will always perform well; if an investment posts a loss, they conclude it was a bad investment. *They need to be told that no investment does well all the time*—that's a major reason diversification is so important.

4. Teach participants to evaluate risk in personal terms.

"Nobody can invest in a vacuum," says William Arnone, a principal at Buck Consultants. "People have to know, 'What am I investing this dollar for? Retirement? An emergency fund? To buy a house? To pay for my kids' education?'"

Most 401(k) plan participants are investing for their retirement, but many also intend to use this money to pay for shorter-term expenses such as college tuition or the purchase of a home. Robert Wuelfing, President of ARI, suggests that a good educational program should include a questionnaire that helps participants determine their own financial needs and identify which investments best fit their personal goals.

Conventional wisdom, he points out, says that young plan participants should invest most of their retirement accounts in equities. But a good education plan doesn't simply parrot conventional wisdom; it acknowledges employees' real life concerns. It may be appropriate for some young participants to allocate a larger share of their assets to stable value funds than conventional wisdom would suggest—if, for example, they are worried about their job security and lack any other savings.

"The 20-year numbers show that stocks earn a bigger return than fixed-income investments, but the average employment today lasts about seven years," Wuelfing points out. Employees may not intend to spend their 401(k) savings before they retire, but those who want to preserve their ability to tap these savings before retirement—if they have to—should have some 401(k) money in low-risk funds.

---

[9] In June 1995, the SEC approved a one-year trial of a new, short fund prospectus called a fund profile. It includes a bar chart illustration that shows how the fund has performed each year, including years of losses. Currently, many prospectuses contain bar charts that illustrate how much an investment in the fund would have grown over a 10-year period, but don't show years of losses along the way. The fund industry favors adoption of the new bar chart as a standard form of risk disclosure. One way to explain the disparity between the stock market's short-term volatility and long-term predictability: when you travel by car, the fastest route to your ultimate destination may be a road that winds, temporarily taking you in the opposite direction.

THE CHALLENGE FOR DEFINED CONTRIBUTION PLAN SPONSORS
AND PROVIDERS TODAY IS TO COMPLETELY RETHINK
PLAN COMMUNICATIONS AND EMPLOYEE EDUCATION.
EMPLOYEES NEED TO TAKE CONTROL OF
THEIR FINANCIAL FUTURE AND MAKE
SOUND RETIREMENT DECISIONS.

EDUCATE
COMMUNICATE

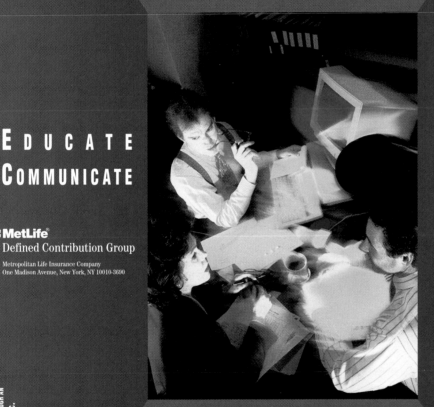

FOR INFORMATION ABOUT
OUR SERVICE GUARANTEE
AND METASSURE[SM],
CALL GARY LINEBERRY AT
1-800-722-6091.

METLIFE REDEFINES FULL SERVICE DEFINED
CONTRIBUTION PLAN COMMUNICATIONS WITH
INTEGRATED PLAN SPONSOR ADMINISTRATION SUPPORT.
DEDICATED ENROLLMENT AND CLIENT SERVICE TEAMS
EDUCATE AND COMMUNICATE WITH PARTICIPANTS. IT'S
GOOD FOR YOUR EMPLOYEES. VERY GOOD FOR YOUR COMPANY.

Some plan sponsors go out of their way to provide information that helps employees see investing in personal terms. Public Service Electric & Gas provides a personal annual benefits statement with graphs and charts that is customized for each employee. "The statement says, based on what you're doing now, here's your income replacement ratio when you're 65 and here are the components that make it up: pension, Social Security, 401(k)," explains Richard Quinn, Manager of Benefits Planning. "If you increase 401(k) savings by 1%, here's what it would do to your income in retirement."

Kroger also supplies detailed benefits statements to its participants. "They definitely increase participation and we've seen an increase in savings rates, too. People can only understand real dollars," says Conley. "A detailed annual statement gets them to focus on how they're doing. Sure, they can call an 800 number and get a projection, but they'll have no idea how they got that number. If you give them a one-page spread sheet showing the beginning balance, their yearly contribution and the company's match, compounding year by year, you initiate a personalized education and they take the information away with them."

5. Stress the importance of devising a basic investment strategy that will meet specific dollars and cents goals.

Many participants lack confidence in their investment management ability because they have no strategic plan to reach their goals; they invest in whatever is popular among their friends or applauded by the media for earning record returns. When the stock market falls, people who bought equities as part of a long-term asset allocation strategy are much less liable to panic or feel they made the wrong decision than are those who bought stocks because everybody said the market was the hot place to be.

An investor with a carefully thought-out strategy is more likely to pause and consider whether the strategy is still valid before rushing to cash out. That important pause for reflection can be very reassuring. As Peter Lynch explained: "When another crash like '87 comes along and your Dunkin' Donuts stock goes down, you can ask yourself, 'Is the company threatened by low-cost Korean imports of doughnuts? Are people going to drink less coffee because the market crashed?' No, of course not, so this is a chance to buy more stock at bargain prices."[10]

LOOK AT YOUR COMPANY'S DB PLAN: IT'S A GOOD EXAMPLE OF ASSET ALLOCATION

Nothing makes the point as effectively to plan participants as an example close to home. In a mid-1995 pilot program it intends to expand, Kroger illustrated the importance of long-term strategies like asset allocation and diversification by showing employees how the company invests its defined benefit plan assets and telling them, "You might not have the same time horizon as the DB plan, but you

---

[10] Press conference, New York City, February 27, 1989.

METLIFE'S DEFINED CONTRIBUTION PROGRAMS GO BEYOND INITIAL ENROLLMENTS.

WE FOCUS ON SUSTAINED ENROLLMENTS THROUGH EDUCATION,

GETTING EMPLOYEES INTO YOUR PLAN AND KEEPING THEM THERE. OUR STRATEGIC APPROACH TO COMMUNICATION AND EDUCATION CAN BE TAILORED TO YOUR

E D U C A T E

COMMUNICATE

MetLife
Defined Contribution Group

Metropolitan Life Insurance Company
One Madison Avenue, New York, NY 10010-3690

FOR INFORMATION ABOUT
OUR SERVICE GUARANTEE
AND METASSURE[SM],
CALL GARY LINEBERRY AT
1-800-722-6091.

EMPLOYEES' UNIQUE NEEDS, ENSURING COMPREHENSION INSTEAD OF CONFUSION. OUR COMMUNICATION CONSULTANTS MONITOR YOUR PLAN TO KEEP IT ON TRACK.

THIS UNIQUE APPROACH IS BACKED BY METASSURE[SM],

METLIFE'S NEW PARTICIPATION GUARANTEE PROGRAM.

"How many of you feel that at least 25% of your employees understand how much money they will need in retirement?'

have a long horizon and maybe you can learn something from the investment strategy that has worked so well in the company pension plan."

Kroger decided to use its DB plan as an example partly because a year after adding four new investment options to its 401(k) plan, it found employees still weren't diversifying their investments. The company showed employees how differently the two plans' assets were allocated. It was eye-opening for people to see that in the DB plan, 22% of the assets are internationally invested, while in the 401(k) plan, the international fund has only 1% of assets.

MEETING INDIVIDUAL NEEDS THROUGH ONGOING EDUCATION

Kroger understands that educating employees about risk is a continuous process that needs constant upgrading. Most importantly, it has learned that a single message to all employees isn't very effective. Its 1995 pilot programs are being used to identify the most effective communications methods for different groups of employees. These three sets of pilot programs were designed to increase plan participation, savings rates and investment diversification; each will be expanded or reconfigured after the company assesses its results.

The first program targeted employees who have been eligible to join the company's 401(k) plan for at least three years but who still don't participate. Recognizing that these eligible enrollees would respond best to very individual attention, the program was developed essentially as "a personalized re-enrollment campaign," says Conley. The company did individual projections showing non-participants how much a 2% or 3% of salary annual contribution could be worth to them by age 65 and how such a contribution would affect their take-home pay.

Meetings for non-participants featured testimonials from co-workers who do participate in the plan.

The second pilot program aimed at participants who save less than 5% of their gross pay every year. Participants were encouraged to save more through specific examples. Personalized projections were made for each of these employees showing how small increases in their contributions can make a big difference to the amount of their total assets over the long-term—even if they increase their contributions by just one or two percentage points every year.

The third pilot program focused on teaching participants the importance of asset allocation and diversification. It targeted employees who had participated in the plan for at least ten years and/or had account balances that exceed their annual salaries. This program's goal was to teach these participants how to use basic investment strategies to increase their long-term investment returns.

The Kroger pilots demonstrate a growing trend in 401(k) investment education: plan sponsors are targeting their message to different employee groups in response to their specific investment behavior. Such a customized approach enables employers to achieve a level of personal communication with their participants that, without computer technology, would have been impossible even a few years ago. Indeed, tailoring their messages to various audiences helps plan sponsors meet their employees' individual needs for investment education more effectively—and employees, responding to that effort, often make larger and wiser plan contributions.

An ongoing educational program that recognizes and responds to plan participants' real investment behavior is the best tool employers can provide to help their employees master the task of managing their own retirement accounts.

401(K) ⓒ OMPLETE

It's about people

401(K) COMPLETE℠ SERVICES

Investment Options from MainStay and other Fund Families*
Employee Communications and Education
Participant Service Center
Recordkeeping and Administration
Plan Design and Consulting
Trustee Services

Younger people. Older people. People with diverse retirement needs. Your 401(k) plan has to work for all employees by providing an easy way for them to understand what your plan is all about. And how to get the most from it.

After all, a 401(k) plan isn't about numbers.

It's about people.

NYL Benefit Services Company
A New York Life Company

Call 1-800-586-1413

PICTURES OF RISK FOR THE DC INVESTOR

Drew W. Demakis
Ruth Hughes-Guden

M any employees, preoccupied with protecting their DC assets from loss or diminution, struggle with persistent fears about investment risk. How can you allay their fears and explain the concepts of investment risk?

This chapter includes illustrations and examples of investment risks that will help you answer employee questions and alleviate their confusion. It explains the primary types of risks affecting DC investors, suggests tools they can use to manage those risks and summarizes the significant, and sometimes overlooked, benefits of DC plans.

PRIMARY RISKS FACING THE DC INVESTOR:

VOLATILITY

Any explanation of risk should begin with an explanation of volatility which, as measured by standard deviation, is the form of risk most frequently measured by practitioners.

In investment portfolios, standard deviation measures the dispersion of returns of a particular investment over time against its long-term average. Standard deviation conveys the probability of returns falling within a specific range. As illustrated in **Figure I,** a portfolio with an average annual return of 10% and a standard deviation of 15% can be expected to have a return between -5% (10% minus 15%) and 25% (10% plus 15%) roughly two-thirds of the time. 95% of the time, return can be expected to fall within 2 standard deviations of the mean (between -20% and +40%). When comparing two investments, the one with the lower standard deviation is said to be less risky.

The second step in educating employees about volatility requires a description of the history of volatility versus return for the major asset classes. **Figure II** shows average returns and standard deviations for a series of common indices for the period from 1926 to 1994 (the longest history for which data is available). The chart shows clearly the positive relationship between risk (standard deviation on the horizontal

FIGURE I

VOLATILITY WITHIN A NORMAL
DISTRIBUTION OF INVESTMENT RETURNS

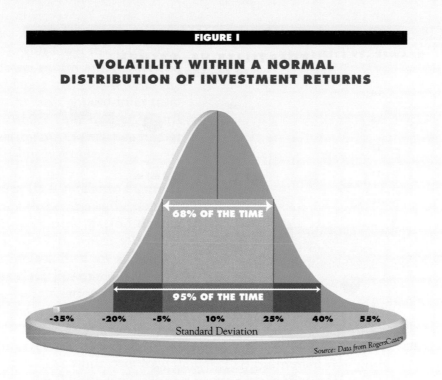

68% OF THE TIME

95% OF THE TIME

-35%   -20%   -5%   10%   25%   40%   55%

Standard Deviation

Source: Data from RogersCasey

FIGURE II

VOLATILITY VS. RETURN
1926-1994

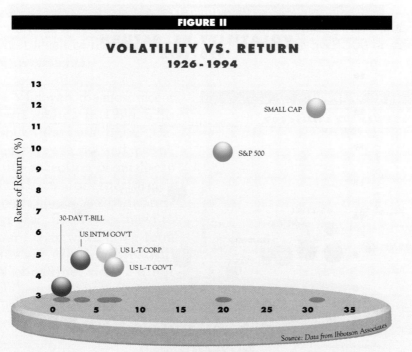

Rates of Return (%)

13
12   SMALL CAP
11
10   S&P 500
9
8
7
6   30-DAY T-BILL
     US INT'M GOV'T
5   US L-T CORP
4   US L-T GOV'T
3

0   5   10   15   20   25   30   35

Source: Data from Ibbotson Associates

Risk (Standard Deviation)%

33

DOWNSIDE RISK

One measure of risk most DC investors intuitively understand is downside risk. Employees are naturally concerned about the need to maintain a minimum level of assets to preserve their living standards in retirement. What most employees do not know, however, is how infrequently major market declines occur, and how the recovery period affects their investment horizon. They should also understand that, historically, relatively short recovery periods follow major market declines and investment returns usually regain momentum quickly.

Table I illustrates the experience of market declines, with examples from the five worst bear markets in history. There are several points worth noting in this data. Three of the five bear markets occurred in the period of the Great Crash of 1929 and the Depression years which followed. Each of the five major declines occurred rather rapidly relative to the time it took to recover (on average it took 2.3 times as long to recover as the length of the bear market). While the times to recover were as long as 15 years (1929-1944), as we will see in later sections, these periods fit within the long time horizon of most DC investors. The most recent market decline—the Crash of 1987—required only 20 months to recover fully to the market peak. A simple remedy for downside risk is to create awareness of its possibility so that, if experienced, any tendency to panic can be avoided.

TABLE I - BIGGEST BEAR MARKETS: 1926-1994			
	MAGNITUDE OF DECLINE	LENGTH (MONTHS)	TIME TO RECOVERY (MONTHS)
1. SEPTEMBER 1929 TO JUNE 1932	-83%	103	184
2. MARCH 1937 TO MARCH 1938	-50%	13	84
3. JANUARY 1973 TO DECEMBER 1974	-37%	24	41
4. SEPTEMBER 1987 TO NOVEMBER 1987	-30%	3	20
5. SEPTEMBER 1932 TO FEBRUARY 1933	-30%	6	8

Source: RogersCasey

THE RISK OF MARKET TIMING

Some employees who begin to understand how the markets work believe they can manage downside risk by timing their exposures to particular asset classes. To them, it seems plausible that they can be in those asset classes that are going up and out of those that are declining. This market timing strategy is attempted by many and mastered by few: 401(k) investors who regularly change their asset allocation mix often damage their long-term returns.

Table II illustrates both the perils and rewards of market timing: for the 25-year period from 1970 to 1994, the best and the worst 10 and 20 months of market performance are alternately excluded. One might assume that missing the best 10 months out of 300 would not impact an employee's portfolio but, in fact, the employee would have sacrificed nearly half the return of the S&P 500.

Note, as well, that for professional investors there is a proportional advantage to successful market timing—avoiding the 10 worst months. Excluding this small number of months, either positive or negative, has a large effect on the long-term result because markets often move very rapidly. For instance, the best 10 months in the post-1969 period had an average return of 12.2%, while the worst 10 months averaged -10.5%.

TABLE II - PERILS OF MARKET TIMING: CONSEQUENCES OF MISSING THE BEST AND WORST MONTHS 1970-1994	
S&P 500 RETURN	11.0%
EXCLUDING WORST 10 MONTHS	16.1
EXCLUDING WORST 20 MONTHS	19.1
EXCLUDING BEST 10 MONTHS	6.0
EXCLUDING BEST 20 MONTHS	2.8

Source: RogersCasey

An employee should draw two key lessons from this table. First, the 11% S&P return over the period is probably sufficient to meet their retirement needs. Second, the cost of missing the best months is so great, they should resist the temptation to practice market timing.

PURCHASING POWER RISK

The form of risk most frequently overlooked by a DC investor is purchasing power risk. Most DC investors do not recognize the need to grow assets in real (inflation-adjusted) terms in order to maintain the purchasing power of their savings in retirement. **Figure VII** illustrates the importance of purchasing power risk to the DC investor. In this example, a participant contributes 6% of pay each year beginning at age 25. Pay rises annually in step with 4% inflation. The chart shows the value accumulated by the participant under two investment scenarios.

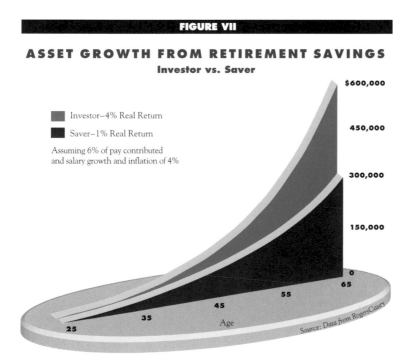

FIGURE VII

ASSET GROWTH FROM RETIREMENT SAVINGS
Investor vs. Saver

Investor–4% Real Return

Saver–1% Real Return

Assuming 6% of pay contributed
and salary growth and inflation of 4%

Source: Data from RogersCasey

37

The first scenario, labeled "Saver", shows a 1% return after inflation (real return) each year, while the other, labeled "Investor", shows a 4% real return. At age 65, the "Investor" has a $600,000 balance—roughly twice the assets of the "Saver". More important, the price of goods in that time frame has multiplied almost five-fold (as seen in the final salary of $96,020 compared with the initial salary of $20,000). The "Saver" will begin retirement with a DC plan balance which is only three times his or her final salary, while the "Investor" will have a balance which is more than six times his or her final salary. This example illustrates why it is important to earn significant real return if a participant expects to live in retirement from accumulated DC plan balances.

Figure VIII illustrates purchasing power in the context of actual market returns: it shows the growth in real value (inflation-adjusted) of $1 initially invested in either Treasury bills or the stock market (S&P 500) over the 25-year period ending in 1994. Treasury bills gained only 38 cents in real terms (a return of 1.3% per annum) over the period. An investment in stocks gained $2.39 (a real return of 5.0%) over the same period.

Purchasing power risk is potentially greatest for those asset classes which have the lowest risk in terms of volatility. This chart suggests that investments in only those asset classes with significant real returns, such as stocks and bonds, can overcome inflation and ensure the DC investor sufficient savings for retirement.

Tools to Help DC Investors Manage Risk:

Having outlined the different types of risk that affect 401(k) investors, we suggest specific tools or strategies to help them manage those risks. To realize the maximum benefit from each and achieve their long-term saving objectives, participants need to understand these tools and assess how they can be applied to each investor's unique circumstances.

Diversification

Asset diversification—creating a portfolio comprised of many asset classes—is the most powerful risk management tool available to DC investors; until "lifestyle" options were introduced, few participants rarely took full advantage of their diversification opportunities.

The success of the asset diversification return strategy relies on different assets in the marketplace not moving in lockstep. Practitioners measure the return relationship between asset classes in terms of correlation, which varies from 1 (perfectly correlated) to -1 (perfectly negatively correlated).

Figure IX illustrates how assets that are less than perfectly correlated can be combined into a portfolio which performs better than either of the assets does individually. In it, Assets 1 and 2 are perfectly negatively correlated with the same return over 20 years. A portfolio constructed with 50% of Asset 1 and 50% of Asset 2 results in a 32% greater value at the end of year 20. Notice also that the path for the 50%/50% mix is much smoother than the path for either of the assets, illustrating a combined lower volatility. This risk reduction is often referred to as "diversifying away" risk.

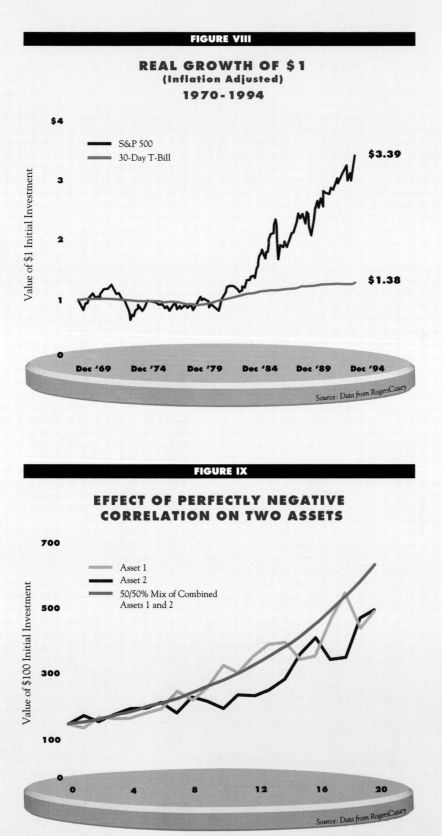

FIGURE VIII

REAL GROWTH OF $1
(Inflation Adjusted)
1970-1994

S&P 500
30-Day T-Bill

Value of $1 Initial Investment

$4

3

2

1

0

$3.39

$1.38

Dec '69   Dec '74   Dec '79   Dec '84   Dec '89   Dec '94

Source: Data from RogersCasey

FIGURE IX

EFFECT OF PERFECTLY NEGATIVE
CORRELATION ON TWO ASSETS

Asset 1
Asset 2
50/50% Mix of Combined
Assets 1 and 2

Value of $100 Initial Investment

700

500

300

100

0

0   4   8   12   16   20

Source: Data from RogersCasey

Years

FIGURE X

THE POWER OF DIVERSIFICATION
1970 - 1994

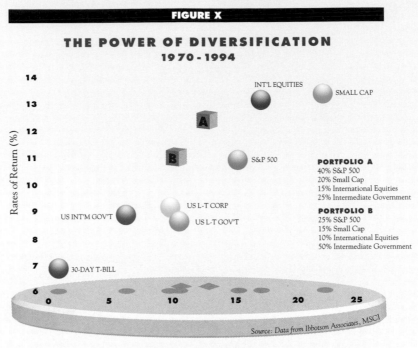

INT'L EQUITIES

SMALL CAP

A

B

S&P 500

US L-T CORP

US INT'M GOV'T

US L-T GOV'T

30-DAY T-BILL

Rates of Return (%)

14
13
12
11
10
9
8
7
6

0   5   10   15   20   25

PORTFOLIO A
40% S&P 500
20% Small Cap
15% International Equities
25% Intermediate Government

PORTFOLIO B
25% S&P 500
15% Small Cap
10% International Equities
50% Intermediate Government

Source: Data from Ibbotson Associates, MSCI

Risk (Standard Deviation)%

FIGURE XI

RISK/RETURN RELATIONSHIPS OVER TIME
1926-1994

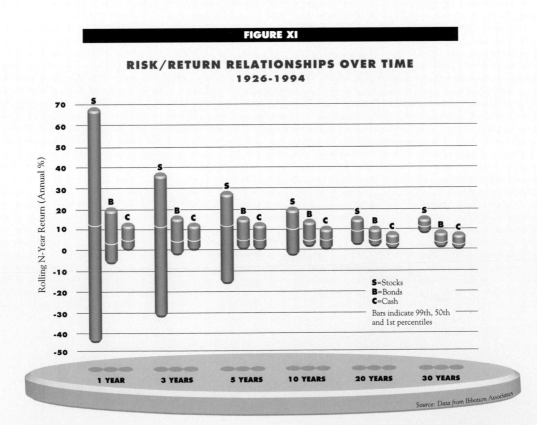

Rolling N-Year Return (Annual %)

70
60
50
40
30
20
10
0
-10
-20
-30
-40
-50

1 YEAR   3 YEARS   5 YEARS   10 YEARS   20 YEARS   30 YEARS

S=Stocks
B=Bonds
C=Cash
Bars indicate 99th, 50th
and 1st percentiles

Source: Data from Ibbotson Associates

In reality, asset classes are not as negatively correlated as the illustration in the previous example suggests. Most, such as stocks, bonds and short-term investments, tend to be at least modestly positively correlated. While this fact limits the benefit of diversification, it nonetheless remains a powerful tool for the investor, as illustrated in **Figure X**. This chart repeats the data from **Figure III**, adding two composite portfolios constructed from the original representative indices.

Note how each of the composite portfolios in this exhibit produces an average return higher than do single indices with similar risks. The higher returns translate into greater compound growth in assets. For instance, Portfolio A would have earned 1% more per annum than the S&P 500 over the same 25-year period, leading to a final value 26% greater than the S&P 500 at the end of 25 years. **Figure X** shows employees that regardless of the level of risk they desire, they will most likely earn higher returns with a diversified portfolio at that level of risk than with a concentrated exposure to one asset class.

INVESTMENT HORIZONS

In making their investment decisions, DC investors often underestimate the importance of time horizons as a second layer of diversification—time diversification. **Figure XI** illustrates how time diversification works. It shows the median and best and worst results for stocks, bonds and cash over a variety of rolling periods dating back to 1926. (In the charts, the red area designates the low end of returns; the blue area designates the high end of returns; the area where blue and red meet indicates the median of returns.)

Note that stocks have had a wide dispersion in returns for periods as short as one year, ranging from a high of 68% to a low of -46%. As the time period lengthens, the returns for stocks shrink dramatically but still outperform the other two asset classes: at the end of 20 years, the worst performance for stocks is better than the worst performance for bonds or cash. At the end of 30 years, the worst performance for stocks is still better than the best performance for either bonds or cash.

As this data suggests, employees with long time horizons can afford to have the majority of their assets in equities. Almost all 401(k) investors should have long investment horizons sufficient to tolerate a reasonable amount of equity risk. Even those approaching retirement need to consider investment horizons and equity investing; if both partners in a couple retire at age 65, they can expect that at least one of them will have to live on their retirement savings until age 86.

DOLLAR COST AVERAGING

Another risk management tool available to, but often overlooked by, DC investors is dollar cost averaging—a form of contrarian investing in which constant dollar invest-

FIGURE XII			
DOLLAR COST AVERAGING			
MONTH	SHARE PRICE	MONTHLY $ INVESTED	# SHARES PURCHASED EACH MONTH
JANUARY	$5.00	$500	100.0
FEBRUARY	$4.00	$500	125.0
MARCH	$3.50	$500	142.9
APRIL	$3.00	$500	166.7
MAY	$3.75	$500	133.3
JUNE	$5.00	$500	100.0
TOTAL	$4.04*	$3,000	767.9

*Average share price during the six months: $4.04 = ($24.25 ÷ 6 months)
*Average cost for your shares: $3.91 = ($3,000 ÷ 767.9 shares)
When you invest the same amount every month regardless of whether the market is up or down, your money automatically buys more shares when the price is low and fewer shares when the price is high.
Source: **Building Your Nest Egg with Your 401(k)**, Investors Press, 1995, p. 35.

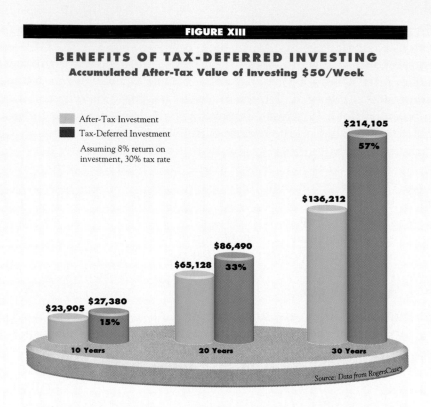

FIGURE XIII

BENEFITS OF TAX-DEFERRED INVESTING
Accumulated After-Tax Value of Investing $50/Week

- After-Tax Investment
- Tax-Deferred Investment

Assuming 8% return on investment, 30% tax rate

$214,105
57%

$136,212

$86,490
33%

$65,128

$23,905 $27,380
15%

10 Years   20 Years   30 Years

Source: Data from RogersCasey

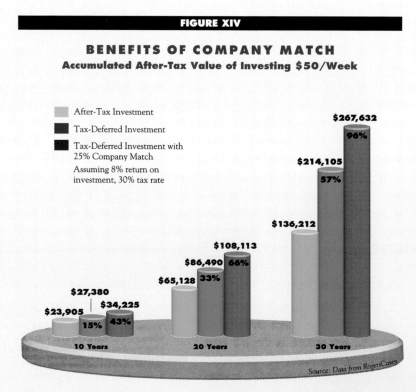

FIGURE XIV

BENEFITS OF COMPANY MATCH
Accumulated After-Tax Value of Investing $50/Week

- After-Tax Investment
- Tax-Deferred Investment
- Tax-Deferred Investment with 25% Company Match

Assuming 8% return on investment, 30% tax rate

$267,632
96%

$214,105
57%

$136,212

$108,113
66%

$86,490 33%

$65,128

$27,380 $34,225
$23,905 15% 43%

10 Years   20 Years   30 Years

Source: Data from RogersCasey

42

ments are made periodically, regardless of the change in value of the investment; more units are purchased when prices are low than when they are high. 401(k) plans, which typically have constant periodic contributions, deliver an obvious benefit from dollar cost averaging, particularly in the early years when contributions are substantial relative to the employee's accumulated balance. Employees can best take advantage of dollar cost averaging by maintaining a consistent rate of contributions regardless of market movements.

Figure XII, on page 36, demonstrates the way dollar cost averaging works.

TAX-DEFERRED COMPOUNDING

401(k) plan investors have a powerful tool in their ability to compound the growth of their assets on a tax-deferred basis. Although this benefit applies regardless of the employee's risk/return posture and encourages equity investing, employees often overlook it because it is most powerful over extended time periods.

Figure XIII illustrates the benefit of tax-deferral through a hypothetical example in which $50 is invested each week at an assumed return of 8%. It shows the results of investing on a solely after-tax basis (with tax paid each year on contributions and gains for that year) compared with contributions and gains (untaxed until the end of the period). In both cases, a flat tax rate of 30% is assumed.

At 10 years the accumulated value of the tax-deferred investments is 15% higher than the after-tax investment; it grows to 33% at 20 years and to 57% at 30 years. Tax-deferred investing brings higher returns because it keeps more assets invested: funds are not siphoned off to pay taxes in intervening years. Given the advantages of tax-deferral, employees should consider concentrating their savings in their DC plan.

Because the rate of return on the assets affects the value of assets invested, the higher the rate of return the larger the impact of tax-deferral. For instance, if in **Figure XIII** the assumed rate of return rose from 8% to 10%, the advantage of tax-deferral after 10 years would help generate a 19% return, growing to 44% after 20 years and to 79% after 30 years. The tax-deferred nature of 401(k) plans encourages participants to accept more risk to achieve higher returns. Employees who maintain both taxable and tax-deferred savings can take more risk with the tax-deferred portion of their assets.

COMPANY MATCH

For many employees the tax-deferral advantage of the 401(k) plan is further enhanced by a company match. While most employees recognize the direct benefit of having the extra compensation from a company match, a surprising number do not take full advantage of this benefit. **Figure XIV** expands the data in **Figure XIII** by adding a third comparison: a 25% company match to the tax-deferred contributions. If you compare the after-tax investment and the tax-deferred investment including the company match, you see that the balance would be 43% greater after 10 years, growing to 66% after 20 years and to 96% after 30 years. The compounded benefits of both tax-deferral and a company match should provide significant incentive for employees to maximize the earnings potential of their 401(k) plans.

EARLY CONTRIBUTIONS

Many younger employees see retirement as a very distant event and are reluctant to save money early in their working careers. While this behavior may be understandable, younger employees must be made aware of the overwhelming cost of not saving. **Figure XV** compares two employees who begin contributing to their DC plan at different ages.

Both contribute 6% of their salary and earn 8% annually on their investments. The employee who begins contributing at age 25 builds a retirement nest egg that is more than twice as large as that of the employee who begins contributing at age 40. The difference results from the power of compounding over a longer period. For instance, $1 contributed at age 25 compounded at 8% reaches $3.17 by age 40. While it is never too late to take advantage of the benefits of 401(k) investing, the earlier an employee begins contributing, the more powerful the advantages and the greater the returns.

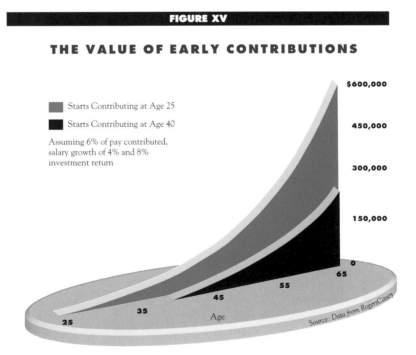

FIGURE XV

THE VALUE OF EARLY CONTRIBUTIONS

Starts Contributing at Age 25

Starts Contributing at Age 40

Assuming 6% of pay contributed, salary growth of 4% and 8% investment return

$600,000

450,000

300,000

150,000

0

65

55

45

35

25

Age

Source: Data from RogersCasey

Of all the places people choose for their retirement, this is one of the most popular.

As one of the nation's largest institutional investment managers, there isn't a more desirable place for your company's 401(k) plan than The Prudential. Fifty million Americans know and trust us for financial and employee benefit services, which goes a long way toward increasing employee participation in your retirement plan.

Of course, employee acceptance alone doesn't account for $33 billion in defined contribution assets. That took time; we're in our fourth decade as a DC manager.

With more than $191 billion in assets under management, The Prudential is one of the nation's largest investment managers..

Jennison and other specialty managers offer diversification and institutional investment management expertise.

It took investment experience, as exemplified by our top institutional investment managers, such as Jennison Associates. And it took innovation in recordkeeping, like an imaging system that gives service reps on-line access to every piece of correspondence in a participant's file – originals, within seconds. All of which makes the journey to retirement smoother for everyone, and The Prudential a comfortable place to retire indeed. For a free brochure on The Prudential 401(k) plan, contact your Prudential representative or call 1-800-862-3344. **The Prudential 401(k)**

Over 50 million Americans trust The Rock to help them reach their financial goals.

Prudential Defined Contribution Services

Prudential Retirement Services, Inc. is an affiliate of Prudential Defined Contribution Services.

How to Educate Employees About Investment Risk:

WHAT WORKS, WHAT DOESN'T,
WHAT PLAN SPONSORS NEED TO THINK ABOUT

Risk is the double-edged opportunity that separates saving from investing: inextricably tied to return, it is a key to investment success when understood and managed well. Plan participants, traditionally risk-averse through ignorance and investing inexperience, are often unduly preoccupied with protecting their assets from any capital loss and unaware of the positive side of investment risk. As a result, plan sponsors need to dispel participants' fears and help them understand and manage risk.

Before plan sponsors tackle this important task, however, they face an even more immediate challenge: to convince an alarmingly high number of employees that participating to the fullest in the company's 401(k) plan is vital to their attaining a secure retirement.

But achieving high participation levels alone is not enough: low contribution rates threaten retirement security as perilously as non-participation does. Insufficient contributions and a naive, risk-averse asset allocation can result in an accumulation of assets that is simply inadequate to insure a comfortable retirement. All employees, whether plan participants or eligible enrollees, must learn the wisdom of *saving as much as they can, as soon as they can—for as long as they can.*

Participation and asset allocation problems are not confined to new plans or those that lack comprehensive communications or educational programs. Companies of every size—including those with well-designed plan features, ample investment options, generous company matches, long-term commitments to comprehensive benefits, exceptional defined benefit track records and respected benefits and pension fund administrators—still struggle with what one Fortune 100 company executive describes as the problem of "getting employees to pay attention to what we're trying to tell them."

The message is clear: *before employees can learn the lesson, they must listen to it.* Plan sponsors must communicate and educate in ways that will be received, understood and acted upon.

COMMUNICATIONS VS. EDUCATION

Finding successful strategies to communicate with employees and help them become smarter long-term investors is often complicated by widespread confusion about the differences between "communications" and "education." Although these words are often used interchangeably, they do not mean the same thing.

Strictly speaking, "communications" refers to materials about the plan, or the process of conveying information about it: what's in the plan, how to use it, how it's administered and so on. "Education" refers more specifically to teaching employees about important concepts that apply to their 401(k) plan and underlying investment concepts in general: what is volatility, diversification, time horizon, compounding; why are they important; what is—and what are the differences between – a bond, a stock fund and a GIC?

Although many communications programs include some educational components, a consensus is growing that communications alone are not sufficient to help participants use their 401(k) plans to their best advantage. Increasingly, experts agree, including both kinds of materials and using a variety of approaches in ongoing educational programs are necessary for both plan viability and participant protection.

For sponsors who lack the in-house expertise, resources or time to create and coordinate long-term educational programs, outsourcing may be the answer. Impartial, independent, third-party sources of educational materials can also help plan sponsors avoid potential liabilities that could result from unintentional violations of the Department of Labor's 404(c) ERISA regulations, whose distinctions between educational information and financial advice remain unclear.[1]

More than 40 plan sponsors, pension consultants, education providers and industry and government officials across the country have been interviewed extensively in the preparation of this chapter.[2] While their contributions represent only an important sampling of leading 401(k) thinking, their willingness to share experiences, insights, successes and stumbling blocks about communicating with employees and educating them about risk opens a new window for our readers on what works, what doesn't and what plan professionals need to be thinking about.

IP's Editors

---

[1] For a detailed interpretation of 404(c) requirements and a discussion of potential plan sponsor liabilities, see **A Wing and A Prayer,** Special 404(c) Report, a conversation between Nathaniel Duffield (Halliburton), Rita Metras (Eastman Kodak), Sally Gottlieb (Apple Computer), a DOL spokesman, attorney Luke Bailey and DC educational consultant Brian Schaefer, Investors Press, 1994, pp. 69-79.
[2] See Acknowledgement.

PART

ONE

How To Build A Successful Communications and Education Program: Problems Plan Sponsors Share

Employees Won't Read

Despite distributing materials they consider informative and understandable, many plan sponsors are frustrated to discover that employees often don't read them. Plan sponsors routinely complain about the avalanche of calls from employees who ask the most basic questions—already answered in materials they have in hand. This is a company-wide problem: the 401(k) administrator of a large retailer sheepishly admits that half the human resources staff hasn't read its own 401(k) plan materials.

Geography Gets In The Way

Having employees in scattered locations makes it hard for companies to do much more than distribute written information, particularly to those locations with only a handful of employees and no human resources staff. Logistics are complicated and costs can be high. Is it realistic—and cost effective—to expect a human resources or treasury official from corporate headquarters to make the rounds of all company locations to talk with employees?

Reaching employees effectively is especially problematic for companies with workers in the field, a sales force that's always on the road or employees who are spread around the country. Montana Power is an extreme example: its employees are dispersed over a 400,000-plus square mile service area that includes remote locations where only a few families populate each gas camp. At one facility work shifts run around-the-clock. How do you coordinate a meeting with employees who are off at 3 a.m.?

Difficult Audiences Require Different Approaches

Younger workers don't want to think about their old age; their spending goals are

"Live for today! They're talking 401(k), but have I got a 280ZX for you!"

concentrated on what they need today, not what they might need tomorrow. As Dennis Dunlap, Conseco's Senior Vice President of Human Resources, says: "We're talking 401(k) and they're thinking 280ZX."

Transient workers, like those at discount retailer Dayton Hudson Corporation, don't participate in the plan because they think they'll leave before they're eligible. Dayton Hudson discovered this attitude even among employees *who had already completed five years of service*.

In addition to the young and the restless, employees at the extremes of investment knowledge can be difficult to reach and educate: those who know nothing about investing or financial planning—or who are convinced they don't want to know anything—are usually difficult to enroll. Those who follow the latest hot stock tip probably participate in the plan, but may resist getting the message about sound, long-term 401(k) investment strategies.

ANTI-MANAGEMENT SENTIMENT

Employee suspicion of corporate motives can be a roadblock to participation. Some plan sponsors encounter gnawing employee distrust, fed by lack of information or misunderstanding, that the 401(k) plan is somehow just a benefit to management—a way, for example, "for the company to raise money," especially if the company match is made in company stock.

Major upheavals—lay-offs or downsizing—directly contradict the corporate message that "we're thinking of our employees' futures." As Glen Pape, Vice President of Financial Services at The Ayco Company, an education provider, notes: "When a company announces a 12% layoff of its workforce, it's hardly the ideal time (to expect employees) to focus on the future. Employees can easily misconstrue the message as: 'Focus on the long-term, even though you could be gone tomorrow.'"

Low employee morale from these or other circumstances, such as labor-management strife and chronic wage problems, can also discourage a positive response to plan communications.

Skepticism About Service Providers

Equally potent as an obstacle to participation—or to the full use of the plan—is the often-questioned credibility of service providers, whether justifiable or not. Employees may resist information from service providers who they know can benefit from delivering the message. Do employees trust the recommendation to put more money in stocks when the suggestion, even if it has merit, comes from the plan's equity fund provider?

Moreover, many employees, particularly those working at companies outside major financial centers like New York and Los Angeles, don't relate easily to well-heeled, big city investment managers who lecture them about the kinds of risks they should take with their money—and even suggest how much of it they should save.

The Fear of Future Liability

Until recently, notes Ruth Hughes-Guden, Managing Director of the pensions consulting firm Rogers, Casey & Associates, Inc., employers said virtually nothing about 401(k) investing. "Corporate legal departments were uneasy that everything constituted advice." Today, the picture has changed considerably. The education issues raised by Section 404(c) have sponsors worried about future liabilities: if plan participants end up with insufficient retirement funds they may blame their employer for inadequate education.[2]

Stacy Schaus, a principal of Hewitt Associates, advises plan sponsors to be vigilant about keeping communications objective from a legal perspective. "You don't want to say something is 'low risk'—that's subjective." Even using the term "lifestyle portfolio" may be loaded, note both Carol Leger, Benefits Planning Manager at Digital Equipment Corporation and David Kaiser, Vice President Retirement Benefits, at Nestle USA, Inc. By characterizing certain lifestyle funds, you may actually misrepresent them; sponsors and consultants opt increasingly for the term "pre-mixed" when they describe fund make-up.

Many plan sponsors are extremely careful about how they discuss investment-related risk for fear of incurring any of their own. Many of Hewitt's clients will not use the word "risk" in their 401(k) materials. "Many plan sponsors still subscribe to the philosophy the less said the better," Schaus says, because they believe that even talking about investment risk can lead to participant misunderstanding and invite potential plan sponsor liability. This attitude, however, is fast being replaced by the notion that sponsors may ultimately face more liabilities if they do not provide their employees with sufficient investment education.

Portraying fund performance in plan communications is another difficult issue for plan sponsors. While investment professionals understand that historical performance is no promise of future performance, the 401(k) participant might assume the opposite, hold the plan sponsor responsible for any investment losses and sue.

---

[2] Section 404(c) forbids plan sponsors from giving investment advice: recommending which fund options to invest in, telling individuals what their asset allocation should be and offering any opinions about investment strategy. Education must explain generic concepts and remind employees that the choices are up to them. Any specific explanations or descriptions of fund options become problematic. See **A Wing and A Prayer,** Special 404(c) Report, Investors Press, 1994, pp. 69-79.

CHARGES OF AGE DISCRIMINATION

Employers also face a less talked-about but equally gloomy possibility: the specter of age discrimination charges looms larger as employees nearing retirement age postpone or resist retirement because of insufficient savings. This phenomenon will probably grow as the first wave of baby boomers approaches retirement age and could be exacerbated by a reduction in Social Security benefits—a distinct possibility given current demographic trends. (By 2045, there will be 100 times more Social Security recipients than there were in 1945, a decade after its inception, with only a tripling of the population. The number of people collecting Social Security in 2045 will be 200% of the number collecting it in 1995.)[3]

? Should plan sponsors show an investment's probability of loss and possibly hamper participation?

? Should plan sponsors show expected returns, based on historical performance, and take the risk that employees won't understand that this year's returns may not replicate the history of the past five years?

? If employees sustain losses, will they come back to the plan sponsor claiming to have been misled? (Nestle, among many others, has been careful not to show anything that *might resemble* a guarantee of future return.)

Although some consultants say that 404(c) creates a larger liability than it solves, it has certainly intensified industry-wide concern about employer education efforts. Indeed, according to Bette Briggs, chief of the Division of Fiduciary Interpretations at the Department of Labor (DOL), because so many plan sponsors have found the rule's distinctions between education and advice so ambiguous, the DOL is drafting an interpretive bulletin that will provide authoritative guidance. It will also include examples that encourage, rather than discourage, education programs.

Briggs offers some perspective: "404(c) is in the nature of a defense for plan sponsors." What is often overlooked, she notes, is that "if in fact someone provides education and crosses the line, it doesn't necessarily mean they would be liable. The real question is whether the advice was prudent or not."

Whether or not the DOL's interpretive bulletin successfully clarifies existing ambiguities, hard data about education results is "the only legal protection a plan sponsor has," states education consultant Mel Albin. "That's where information from the recordkeeper, before and after education, can be useful." But thorough education, says Don Butt, U S WEST's Manager of Trust Investment Management, is still the best protection against employer liability. "For the employer, it's a question of which risk to exchange," notes Pape of Ayco. Concerns about risk and the challenges of employee education have also fueled the popularity of lifestyle or pre-mixed funds, which simplify the choices for employees and reduce their need to learn about investments—a plus for employees who aren't interested and a relief to employers worried about legal liabilities. Fear of crossing the line from education to advice has also fueled a growing reliance on independent, third-party education providers.

---

[3] Craig Karpel, **The Retirement Myth**, HarperCollins, 1995, p. 9. *Retooling Social Security for the 21st Century*, Washington, DC, Urban Institute Press, 1994, p. 57 references data from the Social Security Administration.

Management Complacency

Because the 401(k) plan is a voluntary retirement plan option, many companies feel "It's enough that we provide the plan." For those continuing to provide a traditional defined benefit plan, the 401(k) may be relegated to supplemental benefit status, despite the fact that in today's mobile society the DB plan may provide only a fraction of what a DC plan can provide. The 401(k) plan is often considered icing on the cake and not worthy of any additional effort or expenditure.

Some companies, despite lip service to the contrary, emphasize the plan as a savings, rather than a retirement, vehicle. While that positioning may attract participation, it can dangerously undermine the importance of long-term investing strategies and discourage participants from assuming the kinds of risk necessary to reach their retirement goals.

The Cost to Educate Employees

The real or presumed cost of an education program is often the reason why many plan sponsors refuse or are reluctant to provide one to their participants. Some plan sponsors simply feel they don't have budgets adequate to absorb additional costs; some resist passing on additional costs to participants. "A lot of plan costs are already paid by our participants," says Carol Wooten, Dayton Hudson's Benefits Accounting Analyst, "so we're careful about incurring any more."

But the fact is that education programs can be implemented and sustained at relatively modest cost, and many plan sponsors do share the costs of their programs with participants—or at least require them to chip in some token amount—if only to reinforce their commitment. A variety of payment-sharing options is available for those plans who ask participants to contribute.

Lack of Company-Wide Support

The cost of education programs includes expenditures of both hard dollars and significant company time. In some cases, despite approval from corporate headquarters for programs scheduled on company time, department supervisors cannot jeopardize productivity by allowing employees to leave their job-site; this undermines the overall education effort and weakens the ongoing educational process.

Keeping the Human Touch in High Technology

Increased outsourcing has dramatized a growing shift from manpower to computer power in benefits administration, and with it have come many mixed blessings, observes Wooten of Dayton Hudson.

High-tech recordkeeping and voice response systems make participant information increasingly accurate and accessible and allow companies to track participant activity with greater precision. But at Dayton Hudson, moving the responsibility of disseminating plan information away from individual store managers to a centralized computer system has depersonalized the process. "And often," Wooten notes, "what gets people to respond to the plan is the human touch."

"We can't imagine Fidelity providing better 401(k) service to a big corporation. But the way we're growing, we'll eventually find out."

Birgitt Wirth, Benefits Manager, IKEA

◆ ◆ ◆ ◆ ◆

When IKEA went hunting for a better 401(k), they wanted to be sure that they, and their employees, would be important to their new provider. "When Fidelity said they had a division dedicated to small and mid-sized companies, and that we'd be one of their largest clients, their size was no longer an issue," said Birgitt Wirth, Benefits Manager.

This made IKEA's switch to The CORPORATEplan *for Retirement* – an integrated and coordinated service, all under one roof and only available directly from Fidelity – comfortable right from the start. "Fidelity is very customer service oriented. In fact, it's the best customer service I've ever had," Wirth said.

"Fidelity's enrollment and implementation programs were terrific. But their ongoing support and education has been, too. The STAGES® communications program, the Strategy Selector™ Software, the 800 number support staff – all first class."

And you think, Ms. Wirth, even a big corporation wouldn't get better service? "No, I don't. But ask me again in a few years."

Your retirement plan. Our full time job.

The CORPORATEplan *for Retirement* is designed for small to mid-sized companies. It is backed by a business unit within Fidelity whose every activity is guided by a single purpose: to help all of our customers – from the benefits manager to the most recent plan participant – reach their retirement goals. If you want this level of commitment behind your plan, call Fidelity for a free brochure at 1-800-343-9184. Your retirement plan is our full time job.

1-800-343-9184 Ext. 8423

PART

TWO

How to Solve the Problems

While some of these problems may be difficult to overcome, others are more easily solved, according to education providers and plan sponsors who have succeeded in getting the attention of employees and increasing their investment knowledge.

Marketing Your Message Amid Information Clutter

Why doesn't the communications brochure get read? Does it get lost in the mountain of materials employees receive? Why do employees ignore information about a subject so vital to their well-being—one their financial future depends on?

Because there is so much information competing for the attention of each employee, the challenge for plan sponsors is to create materials that grab participants' attention. This is especially hard to do when most employees feel inundated by the sheer volume of information they receive and overwhelmed by conflicting demands on their time. Scarcely able to get through the day's responsibilities as it is, many employees understandably avoid or delay dealing with a subject that tends to make them uncomfortable.

Because of the fierce competition for their employees' attention, the following are helpful guidelines for plan sponsors to remember when they create educational and communications programs and materials:

Design Materials That Capture Readers' Interest and Attention

Employees shut down when they see a drab, institutionalized cover. They're turned off by arcane financial jargon, pages of complicated-looking data or text they simply can't understand.

Ask yourself: are you taking too long to say what you have to say? Are you saying it in a way your readers can't understand? Some plan sponsors get lost in their own prose and end up ignoring the needs of their audience. Equally important: are you creating a "brand identity" that builds your audience over time and makes your messages instantly recognizable?

Follow basic guidelines for successful advertising: vary color and typefaces, create headings and subheadings that are easy to find and break up copy with a generous use of relevant graphics and pictures. Create related sections that can stand alone, as well as reinforce step-by-step learning. Appealing design is critical, but beware of making your materials too slick. Avoid provoking employees, especially those at the lower end of the compensation ladder, into asking "Why are they spending so much money on this stuff when I can't get a raise?"

Even if you produce materials that have terrific design and content, ask yourself if you distribute them effectively. Some companies, like Conseco and Public Service Enterprise Group (PSEG), avoid the competition of office clutter and emphasize the message, "This is for you and it's really important," by sending materials, including videos, to each employee at home.

Understand How Adults Learn

As you develop the content of your communications and education materials, be sure to consider how adults learn. Remember a fundamental point too often overlooked: *some people simply don't want to learn.* It is not uncommon for employees to consider investing as an unnecessary burden. They may think "I don't want to be an investor. I just want to put my kids through college."

Exploit In-House Resources and Talent

Some companies with in-house asset management provide useful models. Bechtel Corporation, with one of the most respected education programs in the country, offers only a 401(k) plan. Its human resources group issues quarterly bulletins with basic investment information and holds forums once or twice a year on the plan's investment options and retirement planning.

Albert Kirschbaum—a senior investment officer with Fremont Investment Advisors, Bechtel's in-house management firm—suggested the company carry the program a step further and involve his department. "After all," he reasoned, "Bechtel has lots of money managers who talk investment strategy all day. Why not share their knowledge with employees?" Kirschbaum wanted a program that would teach participants about asset allocation as well as global market conditions.

It was a comprehensive effort. Kirschbaum worked with 20 employees for six months to create a new participant seminar program which includes a series of monthly brown bag lunch meetings. Although the human resources department doubted that more than a dozen or so employees would show up, 140 attended the first meeting.

Today, the company organizes monthly presentations by Kirschbaum, area portfolio managers and other speakers, including analysts from the San Francisco Federal Reserve. *"Off the Wall Street,"* his one-page paper, complements every presentation with simple explanations of the markets that meet two goals: to explain basic concepts and describe how the numbers fit together. Attendance at these meetings, begun in 1992, remains high.

Kirschbaum constantly analyzes and revises his techniques: In 1995 he introduced videos from the American Association of Individual Investors to help teach investment basics. Bechtel holds company-wide forums via video-conference and audiotapes the lunch programs for distribution to its 70 field locations.

Other companies are also forming internal 401(k) plan management teams. Xerox, with a highly respected defined benefit plan, brought 401(k) education under the auspices of its investment department. Eli Lilly is another example of a company that has blended the efforts of its pension investments and human resources departments to make education a joint project.

Generally, human resource professionals identify their employees' real-world interests and pinpoint things they need to learn; they teach employees, and recognize the importance of feedback. Treasury professionals, on the other hand, can help build a successful education program by contributing their vital investment knowledge.

Track Participant Activity Accurately

Use recordkeeping data, not anecdotal information, to track what your employees are doing. Teamwork between treasury and human resources departments is critical to gather facts like participation percentages, contribution levels and diversification patterns that help you identify your biggest problems and, in turn, enable you to develop the most appropriate solutions.

It can also be useful to separate your employee population into participants and non-participants, survey them and then examine the reasons for non-participation. Do non-participants think they don't have enough to save? Do they understand the plan? Do they resist investment information because they lack self-confidence as investors? Are they disinterested because they're young and find it difficult to imagine retirement—or even think about planning for it?

Ask for Employee Feedback

Both plan sponsors and education consultants believe that employee feedback is tremendously important. Even the act of soliciting input sends an important message about your concern for employee needs. "Talk to them about what kind of information they need," says Leger at Digital Equipment. Betty Meredith, President of Discover Learning, Inc., emphasizes the need to ask employees how they best absorb information. "You shouldn't treat the program like a Model T," she cautions, "where the choices are black, black and black."

Employee surveys must be regarded with caution, however, and a grain of salt: they have their limitations. Responses to questions can be casual and, if you don't set reasonable limits, you may get pie-in-the-sky requests. People might request monthly materials when you currently offer quarterly mailings. Is that a practical plan option? Will more materials actually have a positive impact on plan participation or asset allocation? Will they be read?

To invest wisely

WITH **CIGNA** LIFETIME FUNDS,℠

YOUR EMPLOYEES NEED A

CAREFULLY GUARDED PIECE OF

INFORMATION: THEIR AGE.

AGE-BASED CIGNA LIFETIME FUNDS℠ MAKE DECIDING HOW TO ALLOCATE 401(k) ASSETS EASIER. FOR STARTERS, EMPLOYEES JUST NEED TO KNOW THEIR OWN BIRTHDAYS. FIND OUT MORE. AND DISCOVER THE STRENGTHS THAT HAVE MADE US AMERICA'S THIRD LEADING 401(k) PROVIDER.* CALL 1.800.997.6633.

CIGNA Retirement &
Investment Services
A Business of Caring.

*JUDY DIAMOND 1995 DIRECTORY, PLANS LARGER THAN $5MM. PRODUCTS AND SERVICES PROVIDED BY OPERATING SUBSIDIARIES OF CIGNA CORPORATION INCLUDING CONNECTICUT GENERAL LIFE INSURANCE COMPANY.

Meet the Different Needs of Your Audience

Once you realize there is no "one-size-fits-all" approach for your employees, try to identify the major preferences and needs of your workforce so you can design the most effective program possible. Employees use education only to the degree they're comfortable, so meeting the needs of your particular workforce is critical. Offer substance appropriate for different types of participants: enough meat for those who want it and as little as possible for the others.

Keep the Program Going

401(k) experts unanimously agree that the most successful strategy for plan sponsors is to create an ongoing education program. A leading consultant emphasizes that this is a strategic, not a tactical issue. "It's not a matter of doing a roll-out with balloons, the clown in the cafeteria and then whew, you don't have to think about it any more."

People need time to learn and apply investment principles; they must be encouraged to monitor their account and make asset allocation adjustments when necessary. "It's easy to get the newly enrolled person to respond, but it's hard to get longer-term participants to think about their plans routinely, to rethink asset allocation as their situation changes," notes Kaiser of Nestle.

Moreover, participants and eligible enrollees are particularly sensitive to the company's commitment to the program. "Employees sniff out a lack of effort," says Bechtel's Kirschbaum. "They can tell when your communications are stale and they don't respond. For a program to be successful, you must work hard at it, and all the time. People have to feel it's important to you before it can become important to them."

Avoid Frightening Doomsday Scenarios that Can Backfire

Help employees understand how to use the positive side of risk to generate long-term capital accumulation. As one investment provider's education director notes, "We are very careful about how we talk about risk: we don't want to scare employees into non-participation. Some communications actually threaten employees they'll be eating cat food out of tin cans if they don't start saving 10% of their salaries."

PART
THREE

How To Get Your Employees' Attention

Once plan sponsors address their communication problems squarely, they can zero in on the most effective strategies to increase participation, broaden understanding and motivate employees to change their investment behavior. Both plan sponsors and education consultants agree that the following strategies get the attention of both participants and eligible enrollees.

Illustrate Retirement Alternatives with Hard Numbers

Montana Power Company compiled and distributed a comprehensive retirement study to its executive staff that combined defined benefit, Social Security and 401(k) resources for various age groups and income levels using different assumptions about 401(k) contributions. "It was," according to Matt Fischer, Director of Qualified Benefits, "a real eye opener." Now the company has decided to use it as a tool to help all employees forecast and understand their financial futures by analyzing the results of different investment behavior.

Personalize Financial Forecasts

Plan sponsors can use individual employee data to stress basic investment principles and show employees what their own nest eggs could look like. Illustrate the result of making the plan's maximum allowable contribution with scenarios that vary according to the level of risk assumed. These illustrations show employees what they are currently doing and remind them that they have other viable alternatives.

PSEG employees currently receive a personal statement each year that includes their financial projections, integrating 401(k), defined benefit pension plan and Social Security data. The statement includes several possible scenarios using different contribution levels. Beginning in 1996, every employee will be able to customize these projections by picking their own numbers for percent of pay, investment returns and anticipated rate of salary increases. The company will upload these assumptions and run them with every statement.

"These 'what-ifs' are the most popular thing we do for 401(k) participants," says Richard Quinn, General Manager of Compensation and Benefits. PSEG routinely surveys its employees about how well the company's benefits are being communicated to them. The enhanced statement also asks participants how valuable it is to them. "Employees consistently rank this material as the most important one they receive," Quinn concludes.

Customized scenarios can also be a tool to encourage non-participants to join the 401(k) plan. As an example, in addition to sending them to participants, U S WEST includes non-participants as well, and according to Butt, one recent mailing far exceeded the standard 1% to 2% direct mail response rate: an impressive 15% of the employees who received the customized scenario mailing decided to enroll.

Not all plan sponsors believe in providing individual "what if" scenarios, however. Eli Lilly's Director of Investments, Fred Ruebeck, is wary of violating Section 404(c) by giving employees the impression that the "what if" is a retirement promise. Moreover, he says, "We're trying to give them the tools they need to make an intelligent decision, but we're not prescribing a particular choice. We can't be judgmental; the choice is theirs."

Some plan sponsors share a concern that these "enhanced statements" could mislead employees because they are based on historical performance data.[4] The "what-ifs" illustrated by possible investment returns (e.g., 3%, 5%, 7%), might inadvertently encourage high-risk behavior. "Enhanced statements never describe risk," notes education consultant Albin. "Just showing increased return without showing the corresponding increase in risk is dangerous." Giving projected rates of return is also dangerous because participants tend to fixate on them.

Instead, he advises plan sponsors to keep the emphasis on asset allocation and encourage participants to review the performance of their asset mix quarterly, rebalancing it whenever necessary. Plan sponsors who like the idea of offering projections to encourage greater contributions might consider presenting various scenarios with a range of variables.

BE PROACTIVE WITH INFORMATION ABOUT NEW INVESTMENT OPTIONS

What's the best time to tell participants about the addition of a new investment option or a regulation that could affect the amount of their maximum contribution?

Identifying the optimal time and the most effective medium for your message should be an integral part of your overall education strategy; it will help maximize benefits to your participants and should reduce any anxiety about what these changes mean to them. "Be proactive, not defensive," advises education consultant Albin.

---

[4] An enhanced statement details not only the individual employee's 401(k) account activity, it gives projections as well. Typically, an enhanced statement shows what happens if the employee contributes one dollar more during each pay period, or 1% more than he or she is currently contributing. Some enhanced statements show Social Security benefits the employee can expect upon retirement and, if applicable, the defined benefit pension. These statements are meant to help participants see how much they will have at retirement in contrast to what they will need.

APPEAL TO MANAGEMENT'S SELF-INTEREST

Conseco's Dunlap takes an aggressive approach: he shows management what's in it for them. Because of low participation levels in 1993, Conseco's plan failed Federal non-discrimination tests and the company's Highly Compensated Employees (HCEs) found themselves with 50% refunds from their 401(k) contributions. Now Dunlap emphasizes to department heads that greater participation by their employees will benefit them. He distributes print-outs of non-participating employees to goad management into supporting participation to help prevent a recurrence of plan failure and contribution refunds. (Dunlap's efforts have paid-off: in 1994 Conseco passed non-discrimination tests and HCEs were able to increase their contributions from a 4% to a 7% maximum.)

PSEG sends similar notices for another reason: to foster support of the company's benefits philosophy, which is based on what Quinn calls "real life" issues. By offering employees the tools they need to deal with the problems of real life—not just retirement, but day care, elder care, college and nursing home searches—the company believes it produces a better work environment with fewer absentees and less stressed, more secure, productive employees. Although 401(k) education classes may divert employees' attention from work for an occasional hour, managers know there is a long-term benefit both to the employees and the company. Managers are encouraged to support their workers' participation and to prevent avoidable scheduling conflicts.

APPLY ADULT LEARNING PRINCIPLES

There's little debate about the key concepts that need to be taught in employee 401(k) education. But the key to success, it appears, is as much in the medium as in the message. Some education consultants use the techniques of adult learning derived from the training industry to help participants focus on their personal retirement objectives and then concentrate on developing skills that can help them make the best use of their 401(k) plan.

Meredith of Discover Learning identifies four steps intrinsic to the adult learning process:

 Explain the concept in simple layman's language.

 Associate it with something familiar from employees' everyday experience.
To illustrate inflation, for example, you might compare the cost of a pair of jeans in 1974 versus their cost in 1994, rather than simply explaining the dollar's loss in value.

 Experience the concept.
Try this example to dramatize the concept of inflation for employees: in one hand, hold up the pair of jeans they could buy in 1974 for $15, and in the other, hold up one leg and a pocket—all that the same $15 will buy in 1995.

Test participants' understanding of the concept.
Ask questions that test comprehension: confirm participants' understanding by asking them to apply the concept to their own situation.

Strong Retirement Plan Services

Our name tells you a lot about us.

"*What makes a retirement plan provider exceptional? Solid investment performance is a must – but it's not enough. You deserve more ... a high degree of competence across the board, attention to detail, and a can-do approach. Every associate in our organization is dedicated to providing you with superior investment results and outstanding service.*"

Richard S. Strong
Chairman
Strong Capital Management

Details make the difference.

At Strong, we strive to anticipate the questions you'll ask when choosing a retirement plan provider. That's part of our job – paying attention to details.

What should

you expect

from Strong?

1 **Partnership – Not Salesmanship.** Your plan is supported by a highly-trained team of retirement plan experts – most are CPAs and attorneys.

2 **Open Architecture Investment Selection.** Choose from Strong's family of 100% no-load funds and other well-known fund companies.

3 **Our Best Customer is an Informed Investor.** Our comprehensive "Investing at work" education and communication program is one of our most important services.

4 **A One-Source Approach to Retirement Services.** State-of-the-art recordkeeping – comprehensive communication and education – flexible investment options.

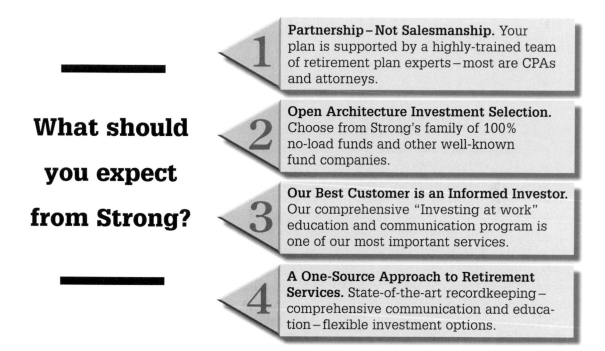

U S WEST's Butt uses "Three Starting Parameters" in the company's 401(k) education efforts:

Multimedia: Use a variety of materials and tools to get attention, teach and reinforce the same message. "Different people learn in different ways," notes Butt. People have various responses to a brochure, teacher, video, software, phone line. They all contain the same messages, stated in different ways.

In addition to many kinds of print materials (enrollment materials, information booklets, quarterly statement stuffers, articles on the plan in the company newspaper), U S WEST's employees have access to videos distributed to human resources people at all locations and the opportunity to attend regular seminars presented by staff. (Butt doesn't use videos at seminars, however; he thinks slides and overheads are more personal.)

Multi-level: Address different levels of education among employees and provide varied amounts of information to make the most effective use of people's limited time and attention spans.

Most employees read at the eighth grade level, a few have Ph.Ds. The problem with many programs, Butt notes, is they are "written at only one level: either they're too basic or they scare the hell out of 90% of your participants." Employees have different investor profiles, as well. Butt divides his employee population into non-participants, savers and investors. To satisfy this diverse group, U S WEST provides a 32-page retirement booklet as well as a less intimidating alternative—a series of seven little booklets. Both cover key investment concepts like diversification, asset allocation and the impact of inflation.

The company also provides a software program that comes with a "road map." Butt likens it to the children's game Candyland: there are many roads to take and places to turn off after five or ten minutes. This provides a "snack lesson": a bite-size concept participants can learn in a spare five minutes.

Printed pieces can be multi-level, too, through the use of tabs, for example, that direct the reader to different "routes" within the piece. Jeff Ross, a principal of the consulting firm Arnerich Massena Education, says it's equally important to design print materials that consider how people read and skim. People ought to be able to read any page of a workbook and come away understanding at least one investment concept.

"Repeat it, repeat it, repeat it." One article on asset allocation in the Fall quarterly newsletter won't do it. Concepts must be repeated, in different ways, again and again over time. Reinforcement also reminds people to monitor whether their investment decisions are producing results consistent with their financial goals.

Bearing the lesson of repetition in mind, Nestle, as an example, shows not only performance results in each quarterly statement, but devotes a whole page to the risk/return characteristics of each fund. Over time, the meaning of risk/return sinks in through these repetitive illustrations, says Kaiser.

TEACHING TIPS

WATCH YOUR LANGUAGE
Write and speak in language that is understandable to line workers, yet won't insult the company president.

AVOID WALL STREET-SPEAK
"Standard deviation" and "R2" are lost on the typical participant; some plan sponsors go so far as to avoid the term "volatility", considering it jargon. Others suggest substituting such fund option terms as "stability", "income" and "capital appreciation" with simpler labels: "cash fund", "bond fund" and "stock fund."

BE CONSISTENT WITH TERMS
Use the same terms throughout your company materials: if "company match" is the term your company uses for company contribution, use only that.

USE LOW SALARIES IN EXAMPLES
This prevents alienating the lower-paid employees and makes it easy for them to see themselves in examples. Higher-paid employees won't be insulted; in fact, they will realize implicitly that their own numbers and results are higher.

KEEP PRESENTATIONS PUNCHY, LIGHT AND, WHEREVER POSSIBLE, FUN.

Other important ingredients plan sponsors use to build successful communications and education programs include:

➤ Self-Paced Learning
Self-paced learning works best in conjunction with live programs. Tools include audiotapes, toll-free phone support, software worksheets—even follow-up "spot calls" from your education provider.

➤ Modeling software
Software that allows participants to model retirement planning options is very popular, particularly at companies where employees are computer-literate. The many easily created scenarios help participants make informed decisions about their time horizons, contribution levels and risk tolerance.

Viewing modeling software as an education panacea, however, can be dangerous. Despite popular beliefs, most people today are not computer literate and many still don't have access to computers either at work or at home. Much available software has drawbacks and can be "a tool in a vacuum": employees don't always understand the logic of how they get from Point A to Point B. Limited software options skew the choices and decisions people make. The result: employees get different outputs with no criteria to measure which is appropriate for them.

➤ Communications Participants Can Understand
Investment managers and plan sponsors are accustomed to lengthy, complex materials packed with statistics, graphs and charts. Education materials for 401(k) participants

require a different approach: simplicity and clarity. Nestle, among others, abides by the maxim that a single picture or graph is worth a thousand words.

➤ Interactive Workshops

A consensus is building that workshops can be the single most effective technique to stimulate employee interest in 401(k) plans. Presentations by human resources and treasury staff, as well as programs developed by outside providers, bring consistently positive results.

U S WEST's treasurer rallied both its treasury and human resources staff to travel throughout the company's service region and talk to employees about the 401(k) plan. Recognizing its importance, Mark Schwanbeck, Assistant Treasurer at The Times Mirror Company and Eric Wood, Director of Pension and Thrift Management at Asea Brown Boveri, Inc., take it upon themselves to travel to company locations to talk about their plans with employees in person.

Some companies offer one-on-one counseling, claiming it's the only way to teach people about their own investment needs. Critics argue that a half-hour counseling session is hardly adequate. Financial planning, they point out, is not a simple process: to truly educate employees, they need multiple sessions, group interaction and a comprehensive program.

The best education programs include different tools that meet different needs. Quarterly performance or factual information can be communicated adequately through only a newsletter or a prospectus. But to encourage a change in behavior and attitude and increase investment skills, workshops are among the best long-term tools.

PAY ATTENTION TO WORKFORCE DIVERSITY AND PEER INFLUENCE

Should plan sponsors pay attention to the educational and cultural differences within their employee population? Whether or not you design materials and programs for specific employee groups, you should acknowledge that differences exist.

Successful plan communications reflect good advertising principles and address the needs and interests of different audiences. Just as Budweiser uses different ads to sell beer in urban areas from those it uses in suburban locales, plan sponsors need to "advertise" to distinct audiences.

Many plan sponsors agree that targeting specific groups of employees is useful in recruiting new participants, urging employees to maximize contributions and persuading them to attend educational workshops. Beyond these areas, however, debate persists about whether plan sponsors should attempt to educate specific groups of employees differently. The jury is still out: education programs are relatively new and the impact of cultural differences on investment behavior is still subject to speculation. Many plan sponsors are considering whether they would help their employees become smarter long-term investors or have greater success in converting non-participants if they segmented their communications and education materials.

> Participant behavior may reflect peer influence: employees who share ethnic, generational or particular cultural or educational experiences often deal with saving and retirement issues in very similar ways. One consultant notes that senior executives at a client's New Jersey location are heavily invested in government securities funds, while their counterparts at the company's Florida location shun those funds entirely.

"If we don't invest in our funds, why should you?"

– Roy Neuberger,
Partner & Founder,
of Neuberger & Berman, L.P.

Forty-five years ago, I became the first Neuberger & Berman mutual fund investor. Today, my partners and I, together with our employees and their families, have over $100 million of our own money in our no-load funds. I invite you to call now and find out about joining us as a Neuberger & Berman investor. I think you'll decide that's a smart idea – even if you're not an employee. Call for a prospectus containing complete information about our funds. Please read it carefully before you invest. **1-800-877-9700, ext. 3670.** Or, on AOL, keyword: Neuberger.

© 1996 Neuberger & Berman Management Incorporated, Distributor.

Neuberger & Berman Funds ᔆᴹ

Anne Lew, Corporate Benefits Manager at Advanced Micro Devices, argues that it's hard to be all things to all people. With participation levels at 80%, cultural differences don't seem to reduce the effectiveness of AMD's education program, but Lew notes that in terms of its format and frequency, coming up with a "common denominator" to meet the needs of a highly diverse workforce is a real challenge. For now, she says, "We take a fluid approach, which really means trial and error." The company views its educational effort as a dynamic process and adjusts their strategy as they go along.

Some plan sponsors and education experts say demographic differences don't necessarily reflect how people feel about risk or indicate their attitudes toward investing. For policy reasons, U S WEST's Butt rejects the notion of structuring an education program according to demographics. He believes that overt segmentation could be perceived as stereotyping—or even worse, as discrimination. From a practical perspective, Butt also thinks the cost of creating different materials and different workshops might be prohibitive and produce only incremental gains.[5]

Some industry professionals say that once you've attracted a willing "student", demographic differences should not affect the learning process. "Cosmetic" targeting, however, may be useful: for those concerned that a seminar about investing basics might not attract more sophisticated employees—or at least those who think they have more investment savvy—Hewitt's consultant David Veeneman suggests offering the same workshop but using different names. "A Saver's Approach to Investing" would draw the beginners; "Principles of Strategic Asset Allocation" would attract the more sophisticated. The content could be essentially the same, but the way the material is presented—the language used, the examples given—might be different.

But as far as the level of content is concerned, it can be dangerous to make assumptions about employees' investment knowledge based on their job functions: the blue-collar worker may actually know more about investing than the white collar marketing manager—simply because he or she wants to.

How well people understand risk also cuts across demographic lines. "What matters is employees' familiarity with investing and their receptiveness to it—and that," Meredith of Discover Learning notes, "cuts across income and gender lines. It's not uncommon for a janitor and a vice president to be in the same seminar group," she says. "Keep segmentation to interested vs. disinterested, degree of saving and investing experience, new vs. long-time participants, undiversified vs. well-diversified participants."

---

[5] It is sometimes necessary to segregate seminars for other very practical reasons that have little to do with cultural issues: different benefits may be offered to different levels of the workforce.

Neuberger & Berman Management is proud to work with the following 401(k) Plan Providers.

Hewitt Associates LLC • Nationwide Life

Aetna Retirement Services • MetLife Defined Contribution Group

Bankers Trust • American Express Institutional Services

Mercantile-Safe Deposit & Trust Co. • North American Trust Co.

BZW Barclays MasterWorks • Abar Pension Services

Charles Schwab & Co., Inc. • Foster Higgins • CalTrust • Buck Consultants

Kwasha Lipton • Northwestern National Life Ins. Co.

Northern Trust/Hazlehurst • William M. Mercer, Inc. • Union Central

Towers Perrin • Howard Johnson & Co. • Chase Global Investor Services

Federated Retirement Plan Services • Sun Life of Canada (U.S.)

Professional Pensions, Inc. • Moyer & Ross • First Interstate Bank

Godwins Booke & Dickenson • Fleet Investment Advisors

We're also proud of our Funds' performance.

Equity Funds Average Annual Total Returns For Period Ended 12/31/95*			
Equity Funds	1 Year	5 Years	10 Years
Guardian	32.11%	19.45%	14.85%
Manhattan	31.00%	16.45%	13.40%
Partners	35.21%	17.31%	13.84%
Focus**	36.19%	19.26%	14.28%

The partners and employees of Neuberger & Berman and their families have over $100 million invested in our Funds. To learn how you can add Neuberger & Berman Funds to your 401(k) plan, call your Plan Administrator, or Neuberger & Berman Institutional Services at **1-800-366-6264, ext. 3674.** A prospectus containing complete information can be obtained from Neuberger & Berman Management Inc. Please read it carefully before you invest. Or, on AOL, keyword: Neuberger.

*One year and average annual returns are for periods ended 12/31/95. Includes reinvestment of all dividends and capital gain distributions. The Neuberger & Berman Equity Funds were reorganized in 8/93. Performance and information for periods prior to 8/93 refer to the predecessor of the Funds. Results represent past performance and do not guarantee future results. Investment returns and principal may fluctuate and shares when redeemed may be worth more or less than original cost. **This Fund's name prior to 1/1/95 was Neuberger & Berman Selected Sectors Fund. Prior to 11/1/91, the investment policies of the predecessor of Neuberger & Berman Focus Fund required that a substantial percentage of its assets be invested in the energy field; accordingly, performance results prior to that time do not necessarily reflect the level of performance that may be expected under the Fund's current policies.

Neuberger & Berman Funds℠

If we don't invest in them, why should you?

DID THE MESSAGE GET THROUGH?

How can you measure the success of your educational efforts? Use the data available from recordkeeping and payroll. Before you begin an education program, download data and establish test and control (those who don't take part in the program) groups. After the program, track changes in participation rates, aggregate asset allocation shifts, changes in contribution amounts and individual activity.

Be sure to revise your assumptions. Changes in a fund's performance must be accounted for in participants' personalized statements in order to provide the information and time necessary they need to make appropriate allocation adjustments.

Try to be patient; give your program time. "One year, even 18 months, is too soon to expect marked results," says Quinn of PSEG.

PART
FOUR

How to Educate Employees About Risk:
Separate the Myths from the Realities

Risk persists as the financial world's scariest four-letter word. Although professionals know that when used wisely it is a vital ingredient that can generate increased returns, the average 401(k) participant most often thinks of risk in purely negative terms. Educating employees about risk—how to understand, manage and use it—is the crux of every investment education program.

Brian Schaefer, President of 401(k) Ventures, sees risk—and the degree to which it is misunderstood—as the key element driving plan participants' behavior. Whether your plan offers eight fund choices or eighteen, most people believe there are only two alternatives, he says: funds that locks in a fixed, predictable return (the GIC, the bond fund) and those that don't and may lose value. "The challenge is to give participants the information that makes them take that leap of faith and accept the fact that over time the funds that don't have fixed returns can reward them more generously."

What information should plan sponsors give participants that will help them see the positive side of risk? A good first step is to separate the myths from the realities:

Myth 1
People define risk as a form of gambling, a black-and-white, win-lose proposition.
Many participants fear that losing all their money is the inevitable outcome of assuming risk. Hewitt surveyed participants in focus groups and workshops and discovered that people steer clear of risk-taking and stick to what they perceive as risk-free options, like GICs.

Myth 2
People link risk only to taking action. This misconception is dangerously deceptive because, ultimately, choosing inaction in 401(k) investing is the riskiest choice of all.

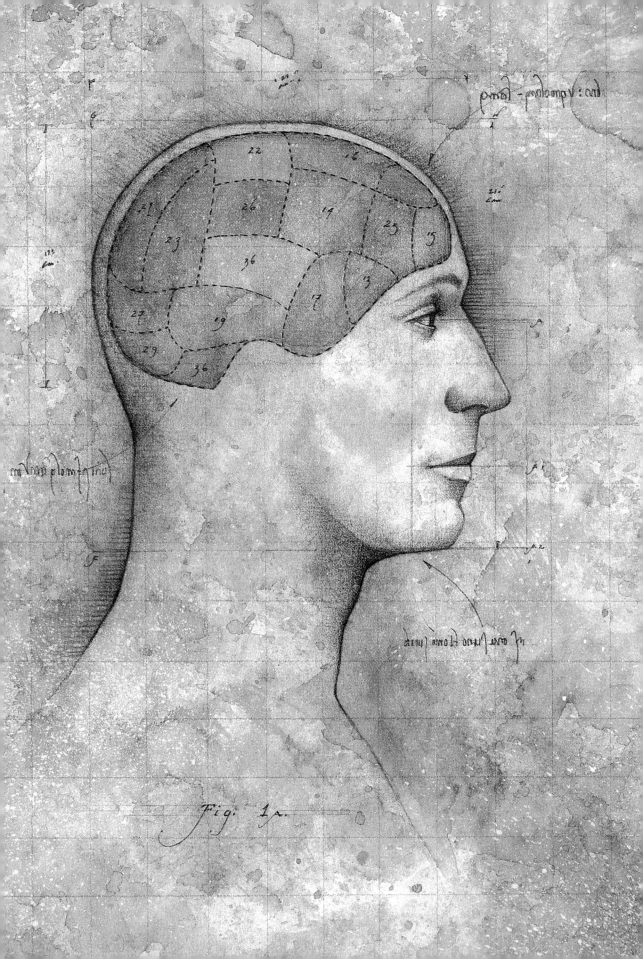

Fig. 1a.

Maybe the time has come to introduce your employees to the most powerful retirement vehicle there is.

It's not a stock. It's not a mutual fund. Nor an exotic new financial instrument. It's knowledge.

And in a time when your employees are dependent upon themselves to make the financial and investment decisions that affect their retirement nest-egg, knowledge makes all the difference.

With this in mind, Fleet has created an employee investment educational program that shows your employees how to build their 401(k) retirement plan around top rated, professionally managed mutual funds, including the Galaxy Family of Funds. This program will educate, train and build their knowledge of market dynamics and risk management. And it's all done with Retirement Plus^{SM}, a package of printed and audio-visual materials that make everything clear, concise and easy to understand.

To find out more, call 1-800-556-7088, and ask for Marshall Raucci, Jr. at Ext. 6518. It's definitely the right call to make if you're looking to introduce your employees to the most powerful retirement vehicle there is.

Fleet *Investment Advisors*

Myth 3

Employees don't understand there's risk attached to any decision they make about their 401(k). Employees should not avoid risk—they should choose carefully and intelligently the risks they will take. They need to learn about different kinds of risk and understand the concept of exchanging risks. For example, "If I put my money into a CD, there's very little volatility, no market risk and no credit risk. But there's lots of inflation risk and opportunity cost risk since, historically, stocks will do better. So, when I say I'm conservative with my 401(k), I'm saying I'd rather accept the risk that I won't have enough."

HOW CAN EDUCATION CHANGE THESE MISPERCEPTIONS OF RISK?

Redefine Risk

Schaefer of 401(k) Ventures believes that getting employees to focus on their financial objectives is the best way to correct these misperceptions. Start by identifying how much money they need for a comfortable retirement, using specific numbers. Then get employees to run through this scenario: "If I put lots of GICs in my 401(k) portfolio, there's a high probability the returns won't meet my objective. Therefore, that approach actually contains high-risk investments. If I add a stock component, there's a lower probability of my not meeting my objective." In other words, Schaefer says, redefine "high risk" to mean "the probability of not meeting your objective."

Reduce Fear of Risk

"Risk is a visceral subject," says Arnerich Massena's Ross. "There are known and unknown risks. People are frightened by the unknown; they attach more emotion to it." When you deal with the subject of risk, he says, the first step is to reduce fear by discussing it in concrete terms. "When you give specifics about possible financial outcomes, employees can more readily accept risk and understand that it's a matter of making trade-offs."

Quantify Risk

Performance is no longer the central concern of only mutual fund investors; all investors, including 401(k) participants, are asking more and more often about how to assess various investment risks. Dramatic losses in 1994 suffered by bond funds with big positions in derivatives or large holdings of emerging market debt were a wake-up call to many that performance cannot be considered in a vacuum and, indeed, what appears to be safe may not be. The reality is that an intensely competitive returns-driven market has forced some funds to venture beyond their stated investment policy into riskier investments.

How can participants evaluate the relative risks among their fund choices? As Nestle's Kaiser points out, "the most difficult issue in explaining the relative risks of various investment options is 'how do you quantify it?'" Moreover, he adds, it's complicated to explain the composition of an investment fund to a typical plan participant. "How do you explain that this stock fund is concentrated in energy today, but in retailing tomorrow?"

Kaiser's concern echoes a key debate currently sparking efforts by the SEC to develop a mechanism which mutual funds would be required to use in their prospectuses to disclose the riskiness of their funds.[6] Investor demand for a standardized risk profile for all funds does not suggest that risk measures do not already exist (there is standard deviation, beta, high price/earnings ratios and stock concentration), but each method measures a different risk and no one rating accurately captures all of them.[7] Given existing limitations, is there a reliable snapshot of risk available today?

Morningstar offers a risk score that measures a fund's downside volatility relative to other funds in its broad investment category (equity, taxable bond, municipal or hybrid fund). It also produces a risk-adjusted performance rating for 3-, 5- and 10-year periods. But for plan participants these rough sketches can be insufficient; the publicly held mutual funds tracked by this service represent only one-half to two-thirds of all the funds offered in 401(k) plans.

What about the other half to one-third of the funds which are privately held or separate account funds—a fact, not incidentally, which has come under increasing scrutiny by industry watchers and regulators as the pool of 401(k) assets mushrooms?

The Institute of Management and Administration (IOMA), which provides 401(k) and other information services to mid-sized and small companies, has developed its own proprietary ranking system to compensate for this gap. It collects data directly from funds based on the Association for Investment Management and Research's (AIMR) Performance Presentation Standards. Issued by AIMR in 1993, these guidelines establish standards for disclosing and representing manager performance for separate account funds, a long-needed tool for pension fund sponsors. IOMA then separates funds into narrow asset classes (small-cap, large-cap, equity, growth, income, etc.) and provides comparisons among these relative categories. IOMA's risk scoring system combines two measures that will reflect any major divergence from the fund's benchmark—the telltale indication of a departure from investment policy.

But averages, too, are imperfect: those derived from various measures still produce different results. Catherine Voss Sanders, an editor at Morningstar, points out that "the problem with all quantitative measurements is that they are backward-looking. You only see risks that have materialized in the past. Also, they don't account for credit quality risk, emerging market risk, derivatives exposure and so forth." This limitation underscores the mutual fund industry's opposition to the SEC's risk-ranking effort: opponents claim that a single "magic number" can only be misleading.

While the SEC won't necessarily mandate a single measure, according to Barry Barbash, director of the Division of Investment Management, it remains commit-

---

[6] The interest in such a risk-ranking system is so intense, the Commission's request for public comment generated an unprecedented 3,700 responses. (Susan Nash, Division of Investment Management, Securities and Exchange Commission, September 6, 1995.)

[7] To illustrate the point: in July 1995 *The Wall Street Journal* asked Morningstar to rank the five riskiest mutual funds by each of six measures: beta (a measure of volatility that gauges the degree to which overall stock market fluctuations impact a fund), standard deviation (a measure of volatility that rates how widely a fund's returns fluctuate from period to period), stock concentration, sector concentration, highest P/E ratio (high price/earnings stocks are those of start-up, fast-growing companies which are prone to quick, rather than gradual, drops in value) and largest monthly loss. There was little overlap among the six lists.

ted to exploring ways to enhance investors' understanding of risk.[8] Moreover, notes Susan Nash, senior advisor to the director, contrary to press reports, the Commission is not restricting its search to a quantifiable measure; it is exploring helpful qualitative assessments, too.

How can investor information be improved and techniques for quantifying risk made more accurate and available to 401(k) participants? One suggestion is to require mutual funds to file their portfolios with the SEC more frequently, increasing the twice-a-year filings now common to monthly or quarterly. Some have suggested requiring funds to summarize major holdings and particularly large exposures to specific industry sectors, countries and markets in plain, understandable language. On the flip side, however: accelerating the reporting requirement to monthly might encourage investors to think even more short-term than they do currently, a result no plan sponsor wants.

Even if the SEC's efforts result in new disclosure requirements for all fund prospectuses and, in the best possible case, if these prospectuses include non-technical, understandable qualitative descriptions, they will not necessarily reach most 401(k) participants since only those plans complying with Section 404(c) are required to distribute prospectuses.[9]

At the least, numerical rankings can't help but oversimplify and at most, they can mislead. Practically speaking, it's expensive and unwieldy to provide meaningful narrative analysis of the total risks to a fund.

The moral of the story: whatever comes of the SEC's and other efforts to quantify or qualify the riskiness of funds, there is no substitute for each investor's close examination. There is simply no quick fix. To understand the true risks of a given fund, investors must do their homework and study its holdings, which can change over time, to get a clear picture of the underlying risks of its assets. Whether or not participants actually dissect each prospectus, they must at least understand general investment principles and the basic mechanics of stocks and bonds in order to assess relative and absolute risks. This, of course, returns us to the central need for participant education.

Beyond what the difficulties in quantifying risk pose for participant education, there is another moral to the story: the risk-ranking problem underscores how critical it is for plan sponsors to consider carefully the risks, not simply the performance, of the funds they select as offerings of the plan. As imperfect as existing risk measures may be, it is still far better to consider them than to rely solely on generic notions of the risk/return spectrum. Simply stated, a bond fund may in fact be riskier than an equity fund if, like those sorry losers in 1994, it contains inverse floaters or Peruvian notes.

---

[8] John R. Dorfman, "SEC May Extend Period for Receiving Comments on Risks of Mutual Funds," *The Wall Street Journal*, July 5, 1995, p. C1.

[9] Jim Klein, a principal of Towers Perrin and the chair-elect of the American Bar Association Tax Section's Employee Benefit Committee, estimates that as of year-end 1994 about 10% of plans complied, 40% "came close," and 20% didn't, but took reasonable steps to comply with the spirit of the rule. Notwithstanding compliance levels, the prospectus requirement remains minimal: the regulations themselves call only for a one-time distribution of prospectuses— when the initial investment is made— and another at any time there is a significant change in the fund's composition.

"They call it the sleep factor, Jane. You need to be able to sleep comfortably knowing that you've made the right investment choices and you haven't exceeded your risk tolerance."

Help Employees Develop Personal Risk Profiles

"Let your sleep factor and your time frame be your guide" is a Dayton Hudson guideline, says Wooten. Instead of categorizing fund options by their degree of risk, plan sponsors should help participants assess their own individual tolerance for risk. This helps participants understand the relative nature of risk, and its relationship to time. A common, easy-to-communicate gauge is the "sleep factor": how much risk can you tolerate in your portfolio and still sleep soundly at night?

Nestle's award-winning **Smart Saving** brochure includes descriptions that are typical in self-assessment materials; employees try to find the one that best describes themselves:

A. "My primary goal is to protect my retirement savings. I am most concerned about losing what I have, and I am not willing to take any risk just to keep up with inflation."

B. "My primary goal is to earn enough on my retirement savings to stay ahead of inflation. I am willing to take on some investment risk to do so."

Or,

A. If I had a choice between $1,000 cash and a 1-in-10 chance to earn much more than that, I'd definitely take the cash."

B. "If I had a choice between $1,000 cash and a 1-in-10 chance to earn much more than that, I'd definitely go for the chance to earn more."

Many experts caution against the superficiality of self-tests, however—especially if their use precedes any investment education. Instant self-assessments can motivate employees to give the answers they think they should give. In addition, most people, especially those with the least investment knowledge, tend to associate risk with one type of investment, such as growth stocks.

When employees are asked to rate themselves as conservative, moderate or aggressive in terms of their risk tolerance, the majority define themselves as "conservative."[10] They may think that's the best test answer, or they may really believe they are, but their behavior is contradictory nonetheless. In fact, notes education consultant Albin, the typical 401(k) allocation is roughly 50% in company stock and 50% in GICs: the highest-risk, lowest-return combination imaginable.

A persistent problem with self-tests is that employees often take them before they understand the concept of risk or have had an opportunity to change their misperceptions. "Until employees understand what positive and negative risks exist, the idea of being 'risk-averse' is meaningless," notes Schaefer of 401(k) Ventures.

Self-tests can also too rigidly define an employee's attitudes toward risk without taking into account his or her investment activity to date. What if a 45-year-old employee's profile shows he or she is conservative, yet hasn't saved a nickel for retirement? This employee, obviously, cannot follow a "conservative" strategy and still meet his or her retirement objectives.

HOW CAN PARTICIPANTS DETERMINE THEIR RISK TOLERANCE MORE ACCURATELY?

Ayco uses techniques derived from game or "mini-max" theory. Employees react to specific hypothetical scenarios to assess their response to the results of taking a particular risk. Visualizing how things could go wrong and what the loss would mean to them can be extremely helpful. The goal is to minimize anxiety and establish higher comfort levels with an investment strategy; it's a variation of the "sleep factor" test.

Ayco's Pape uses the example of an executive with a large position in company stock both in options and in his 401(k). Stock options give him ownership of appreciation but not of dividends. He owns 5,000 shares worth $20 each, at a total value of $100,000. He also owns $5,000 of company stock in his 401(k) account. Assume the stock doubles in price. Now his stock options are worth $200,000 and the company stock portion of his 401(k), owned directly, is $10,000 for a combined value of $210,000. Imagine, if instead of doubling, the stock halves in value. The options are now worth $50,000 and the 401(k) stock $2,500.

How badly does he feel? The loss to his 401(k) might be tougher to accept because it's real money he's already contributed, not an option; he may feel this is a risk not worth taking. The potential upside of $5,000 may not seem great enough compared to the prospect of the loss—both the options and the 401(k).

---

[10] A 1995 Access Research, Inc. "Participant Attitudes and Behavior" study of a statistically representative sampling of 1,100 plan participants who were asked to rank their conservativeness as investors indicated the following: using a scale of 1 to 10, with 10 the most conservative, 30% rated themselves between 8 and 9, or "very conservative"; 18% ranked themselves at 1 to 3, or aggressive; the remaining approximately 50% ranked themselves somewhere in between. While Hewitt has not conducted a formal survey of its clients' plan participants, Dave Veeneman's anecdotal observations during workshops and focus groups tend to confirm these ARI findings. About a third of these participants see themselves as conservative, sticking with GICs and other funds they perceive of as "safe", even when they understand different kinds of risk, including volatility. Another third of these participants behave "conservatively" because they don't understand volatility. Once they understand it, he notes, they readily switch and diversify subsequent contributions.

GIVE YOUR EMPLOYEES
A FLEXIBLE RETIREMENT PLAN
WITH QUALITY INVESTMENTS
AND SUPERIOR EDUCATIONAL MATERIALS.

WATCH YOUR EMPLOYEE PARTICIPATION
AND CONTRIBUTION RATES SOAR.

*The Advantage of Momentum.
An eagle launches itself from the ground
with an upward lunge, followed by a
powerful beat of its wings, and within
minutes can climb as high as 12,000
feet. With more than 50 years of experience in retirement planning, we can
help launch your employees toward a
financially secure retirement.*

*A*s a retirement plan client of Allmerica Financial Institutional Services,* you can provide your employees with a lot more than just a systematic, tax-advantaged investment plan.

You can give them an education in retirement planning, a choice of quality investment vehicles (including name-brand mutual funds), and the tools to make intelligent decisions in selecting and diversifying their investments.

For more information, call 1-800-853-AFIS.

ALLMERICA
FINANCIAL®

ALLMERICA FINANCIAL INSTITUTIONAL SERVICES

WISE THINKING. SOLID SOLUTIONS.

The goal is to minimize the risk in different circumstances. "We believe that when in doubt, take less risk. You can always assume more later," says Pape. Most important, he adds, is to remember that if you assume too much risk and the market moves against you, you may feel really burned. If you lose trust in your advisors and overcompensate by investing inappropriately, it might take you years to regain enough confidence to take risk again. When visualizing possible scenarios, he recommends converting abstract percentages to concrete dollars. "People can accept the idea of a 50% loss, but they can't accept losing half the dollar value of their money."

While admitting "there's no magic bullet," Hewitt frames the risk tolerance question differently. To complement their traditional risk profile quiz, the firm developed definitions of three types of investors, linked to a set of choices that fits each type. This helps direct participants into one of three built-in plan structures: lifestyle or "pre-set" funds, balanced funds or their own mix of funds—according to proper asset allocation guidelines.

 The passive long-term investor. "I am a non-investor. I like the idea of really making money on asset allocation, where you control risk."

Believes in active management, but prefers that it be done by a manager. "I'm not an investment expert, but I think a Wall Street guru can move back and forth among funds and capture better results."

Believes in active management and wants to set his or her own asset allocation. "I feel I am a Wall Street guru."

The Type 1 investors have four pre-set portfolios to choose from, each with different risk/return ratios, created from the company's existing fund options. Type 2 investors have a tactical fund and Type 3 investors choose from among all the funds offered by the plan to "do their own thing."

While self-tests can be helpful, they might be a last step. More important, say some consultants, is to consider offering various savings and accumulation assumptions. This is a complex process, but more useful than simply looking at a subjective definition of risk tolerance as a guide to building an investment strategy.

Since the goal is long-term—targeting income needs for retirement—many experts agree that teaching risk and return can be simplified by offering professionally pre-mixed portfolios composed of funds offered in the plan. Create a matrix of each fund to determine the risk. If all the portfolios are modeled along the efficient frontier (optimizing return and minimizing risk), and all have different risk/reward characteristics ranging from short-term to intermediate to long-term, then the only choice for the participant becomes: how much should I contribute?

Once you've identified your target nest egg—say $175,000 by age 65—you can put in 15% of pay and afford to invest in a lower-risk fund than someone who contributes only 3% of pay. The issue of risk is reduced to how much money a participant can afford or chooses to contribute.

The Power Of Two

401(k)

Creating Infinite Possibilities

Combine creativity with power, and anything is possible.

At American Express Institutional Services, a division of American Express Financial Advisors, we understand that every company is different and believe that every plan should reflect the unique needs of each client.

What's more, we have the strength to turn your visions into reality.

American Express has an unparalleled reputation for customer service in the travel, charge card and banking industry. And, for more than 100 years, IDS has helped clients achieve their financial goals. Today, as American Express Financial Advisors, we have a history of Wall Street investment experience and a main street heritage of innovative products and personal attention.

Together, through American Express Institutional Services, we offer you the opportunity to shape precisely the kind of defined contribution plan you want; with "Smart" Products that can be combined to offer the level of service you need.

Call us soon. Because when you combine the power of two, almost anything is possible.

For more information, contact Ward Armstrong at 1-800-437-0600.

Institutional Services

WALL STREET WISE. MAIN STREET SMART.

Reassess Risk Tolerance

An employee's risk tolerance may indeed be a part of their personality. But it will certainly change over time, as their personal circumstances change or as they become more seasoned investors. Plan sponsors need to communicate the fact that an employee's risk profile is not static: it should be re-evaluated and adjusted over time.

Use Education as an Antidote to the Media

While most 401(k) professionals welcome the increased coverage of 401(k)s and mutual funds, the media often undermines the message that risk is good through its relentless, day-to-day coverage of the markets. Caution participants against becoming obsessed with short-term ups and downs and forgetting the importance of their commitment to a long-term investment horizon.

"As our Director of Employee Benefits, Peterson, you of all people should know that you cannot use the four letter 'R' word in our employee communications."

Avoid Using the "R" Word?

As long as widespread misunderstanding persists, should you avoid using the word "risk" in educational materials? Opinions differ.

Some believe that you don't make anyone more comfortable with risk by not talking about it. "Although our education materials are judicious in their use of the word 'risk'", Hewitt's Veeneman says, "risk is at their heart."[11]

Emphasizing the positive side of risk in education materials helps to diffuse its negative connotation and reinforce the possibility of upside gain. Digital Equipment "never talks about risk without talking about the return correlation," notes Leger.

---

[11] Hewitt refers to risk in its own 401(k) plan materials.

How to Communicate Core Investment Concepts

Do participants understand the difference between investing and saving? Industry consensus says no. Employees need to face the hard truth of the facts and figures: unless they work toward a specific goal, their retirement promises not to be what they imagined. With rising life expectancies, they will probably need more money than they now anticipate. As people wake up to the possible, even probable, retirement risks they face, they are more willing to consider the variety of investment risks that can help them reach their retirement goals.

Most basic investment concepts are fairly straightforward. When presented with repeated concrete examples drawn from their own life experience, most employees understand inflation or diversification, for example, fairly easily. Definitions are similar among companies, although some sponsors offer more comprehensive explanations. The critical difference is how these concepts are presented: do they build on each other in successive communications through repeated emphasis and consistency of format, style, illustration? Most important, do they motivate participants to act?

Some plan sponsors combine investment concepts and plan explanations in the same document. Increasingly, however, sponsors are unbundling this information into two or more documents. Some have even found it useful to produce two varieties of education information: a comprehensive booklet for those inclined to read and the same information divided up into several bite-sized brochures for those with a shorter attention span.

What specific concepts do plan participants need to learn? How can they be presented so they can reach, teach and motivate the widest audience?

THE RELATIONSHIP BETWEEN RISK AND RETURN

The most important concept of all is not risk but the relationship of risk and return. Participants who grasp this trade-off—the higher the risk, the higher the potential return—understand the difference between savings and investments. Then it's just a matter of deciding where to be on the risk/return spectrum, given their time horizon and the amount of money they'll need to live comfortably in retirement.

Covering the risk/return spectrum adequately should be the plan sponsor's main goal in designing the menu of fund choices, but it is sometimes displaced by other considerations. Plan sponsors often select this year's best performers, as if the plan were an investment portfolio. But participants are not money managers and 401(k) plans should not focus on quarterly returns.

That rationale may work for DB plans, where a fund manager might divide the domestic fixed-income allocation among three competing managers, see who produces the highest returns and then shift the whole allocation to the best performer. But how do you explain to employees why you have three similar fixed-income fund options? Plan sponsors should not forget the lesson that asset allocation is more important than choice of manager. Many consultants are skeptical of the plan with 50 fund options, viewing it as a case of unnecessary complexity masquerading as choice.

A popular and effective way to explain the risk/return relationship is to illustrate the concept using graphs developed by Ibbotson and Sinquefield: one shows the efficient frontier, placing asset classes along a spectrum from lowest to highest risk. Another demonstrates how $1 invested in 1926 in every major asset class would have fared over the past 70 years if it had been left untouched with the dividends reinvested—a persuasive argument for the long-term power of stocks.[12]

Xerox believes context is important in illustrating risk and return. Its annual report features a chart of ovals representing each of its six fund options placed in their relative positions on a risk/return axis. The chart is repeated in miniature throughout the report: it appears in every section devoted to individual fund performance, with the particular fund highlighted.

THE VARIETY OF RISKS

There are many different types of risk associated with 401(k) investing. Paramount among them is savings or accumulation risk—the risk of not accumulating enough money for retirement. If there were only one type of risk that had to be explained and understood—everyone agrees this one is it.

Contributing to savings or accumulation risk is inflation risk—that insidious, invisible eroding of the value of a participant's assets—particularly dangerous to retirement security and inherent in fixed-income funds. Understanding inflation risk helps participants understand real rates of return as well: what remains after subtracting the inflation rate from the investment rate of return. To meet long-term goals, investments must be made and risks chosen to insure that principal will grow, otherwise inflation will take its inevitable toll.

To illustrate the impact of inflation, Arnerich Massena uses a bright Bureau of Labor Statistics graphic that shows the dramatic rise in the cost of a carton of milk and a loaf of bread in 1950, 1978 and 1992. In its video, PSEG shows the erosion of a one dollar bill over time with a hand stashing a dollar bill under the mattress,

---

[12] Ibbotson Associates Inc., Chicago, IL.

The Guide That Comes With Most 401(k) Plans.

The Guide That Comes With Ours.

Daily Choice

Choose some retirement plans and they'll send you a book. Choose the NationsBank Daily Choice 401(k), on the other hand, and we'll send you a communications consultant: a living, breathing human being who'll explain the program in a way that all your employees will understand.

That's because NationsBank knows that the more informed your employees are about a retirement plan, the more likely they will be to participate. And we've found that there's no better way to ensure their participation than by having someone on site to educate them.

What's more, our consultants will return periodically to update your employees and answer any questions they may have. So they'll be able to make wiser decisions regarding their investments as a result.

But what makes Daily Choice even better is that this communications program is just part of a superior, integrated package that includes administrative and investment services as well.

To learn more about Daily Choice, call Pamela J. Hubby at (404) 607-4794. And see what a difference having the right guide can make.

NationsBank®
Retirement Services

then lifting the mattress at various intervals to reveal fewer and fewer coins.

Participants must also understand the investment risk inherent in individual asset classes (mitigated by proper diversification and asset allocation). Because the 401(k) is a retirement vehicle, this risk should be the least threatening if a portfolio is properly diversified. This is one point, consultants say, that is not being communicated clearly.

Other important types of risk participants need to understand include diversification, market, interest rate, default or credit and reinvestment risk. In addition, participants should consider tax and loan risks (a combination of savings and opportunity risks).[13]

Explaining various kinds of risk to participants does not have to be complicated. Education consultant Schaefer believes in keeping it simple: "Once you identify what's really high risk (not meeting your objective) and explain the importance of diversification and the power of dollar cost averaging, defining the other risks is secondary."

When defining asset classes, Schaefer emphasizes the importance of context to performance; he feels it is necessary to illustrate graphically what is "normal": what can be expected. In workshops, it's unnecessary to explain all the variables influencing the performance of a bond; the most important thing to know is how a bond works. It's important to know that stocks move up and down, and that generally over the long-term they trend higher. Don't try to explain the behavior of stocks—that's even more unpredictable than bonds, and frequently anomalous (e.g., IBM reported higher earnings but its share price declined).

Nestle's **Smart Saving** brochure walks the participant through personal risk-assessment and every key investment concept, as well as through goal-setting, sound investment strategies for the 401(k), worksheets, a glossary and fund descriptions. **Smart Saving** strategies include diversification, using time to control risk and not timing the market.

U S WEST's colorful **Do-It-Yourself-Savings-Kit** includes a series of brochures describing the plan and basic investment concepts. With its theme of the 401(k) as a "financial snowball", it cites various risks that could melt yours and offers a brief explanation of how to minimize each one.

PSEG's video, **Your Financial Security: The Power is in Your Plans** and its companion booklet, use a sailing motif of charting your course for total financial planning, with the 401(k) as a central component. In concise segments, the video addresses safety and risk/reward, tolerance to risk, liquidity and tax treatment. Savings, earnings and time horizon together dictate the rate of return the investor will need and everything comes down to balancing the mix. Showing various computations, the program teaches that "all it takes are minor adjustments to achieve your goal." It also includes helpful information on identifying and prioritizing goals, identifying your time horizon, estimating future costs of your goals and future value of assets, determining future set-aside needs and at what rate of return and inflation's impact on the dollar.

---

[13] For a complete description of the various types of investment risk that pertain to 401(k) investing, see Glossary of Investment Risks, p. 118.

THE POSITIVE SIDE OF RISK

Explaining key concepts that reinforce the value of *positive risk* is also important.

Help participants consider higher-risk investments.

Higher-risk investments enable participants to contribute smaller initial amounts with the possibility of earning more in the long-run: saving 10% of one's annual income with a 10% return will yield more than saving 17% with returns of only 6%. In other words, teach the lesson that risk can be your friend.

Emphasize the relationship of time to risk.

Risk declines over time. The earlier you start investing, the longer your time horizon and the more investment risk you can take. Historically, longer annualized periods provide greater positive returns.

Set the record straight on volatility.

Volatility—how vulnerable an investment is to fluctuations in value—gets more negative press than it deserves, claim many education consultants. Schaefer notes that "the biggest mistake being made in education is talking about volatility as if participants were managing pools of money and evaluating performance with short-term frequency, rather than their being long-term investors who probably won't touch the money for 20 years."

Although 401(k) plans are retirement plans with investment characteristics, they are too often portrayed, consultants concur, as investment plans with retirement characteristics. The risk for plan participants isn't that the value of their money might go up and down in wild swings, it's that they won't end up with enough of it when they retire. "Volatility is good," says Pape, "it's what gives upside gain."

But especially for 401(k) investors who don't have a 30-year time horizon, volatility deserves healthy respect. Older employees who were close to retirement when their company's plans were instituted obviously have more pressure to seek higher yields over fewer years. It's important that they, as others, understand the distinction between annual and annualized returns: a fund's annualized returns over a 10-year period won't necessarily reflect its volatility during shorter periods within that time period. Funds with similar 10-year performance records could, therefore, have substantially different degrees of volatility, the impact of which can be substantial.[14]

THE MAGIC OF COMPOUNDING

The sooner participants start saving, the more their money can grow. Thanks to what plan sponsors call "the magic of compounding," the longer dollars are invested, the more dramatic the possibilities for total capital accumulation.

It's not hard to grasp that participants with longer time horizons can actually contribute less per month and still accumulate more dollars than those who start saving later and make the same monthly contribution. If a participant starts saving at age 25, he or she would need to set aside only 1% or 2% of pay versus the 6% or 7%

---

[14] See Zvie Bodie, "On the Risk of Stocks in the Long Run," cited in the Annotated Bibliography, for a provocative discussion that challenges conventional wisdom about stock market risk over the long-term.

necessary to reach the same retirement goals if saving started at age 40.

The beneficial effect of compound interest reminds plan sponsors how important it is to motivate participants to start saving early. To drive the point home, plan sponsors often use familiar purchases—a pizza or a movie—to show participants how much more they could accumulate over time if they sacrificed just that purchase every week.

To emphasize the point even more, many plan sponsors use the comparison of two people the same age: one who begins saving at age 25 but stops after 10 years; the other who begins to save when the other person stops. Lisa puts away $100 a month for 10 years (for a total of $12,000) and stops, but interest continues to work for her. Todd began to save at age 35, the time Lisa stopped; he saved $100 a month in the same investments as Lisa (returning 6%), but over 30 years he had to set aside 3 times as much to arrive at the same amount, $100,000.

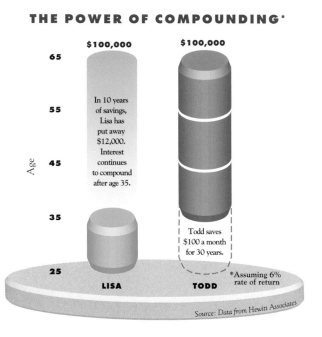

THE POWER OF COMPOUNDING*

In 10 years of savings, Lisa has put away $12,000. Interest continues to compound after age 35.

Todd saves $100 a month for 30 years.

*Assuming 6% rate of return

Source: Data from Hewitt Associates

ASSET ALLOCATION AND DIVERSIFICATION

These are two important investment concepts that are often used interchangeably. Consequently, their important distinction is not always clear to employees. If you divide your 401(k) money among three different fixed-income funds—a government bond fund, a money market fund and a GIC fund—you will be somewhat diversified, but you will also violate the basic principles of asset allocation.

Investment professionals know that asset allocation has by far the greatest influence on investment returns, overshadowing both individual manager performance and security selection. As much as 92% of return can be attributed to asset allocation, a phenomenon Hewitt calls the "Rule of 92". Conveniently, that fact can be the most powerful argument a plan sponsor presents against market timing.

Asset allocation decisions should be driven by the participant's funding objectives. Participants should first anticipate what their needs will be at age 65 and into retirement, and then determine an asset allocation that meets those needs. Clearly, major life cycle events—marriage, birth of a child, a new mortgage, divorce, spouse's death—will trigger asset allocation reviews and prompt necessary changes, but in any case, periodic rebalancing should be made over time.

The need to rebalance the portfolio over time is a point frequently overlooked in basic 401(k) communications. Participants who do modify their asset allocation after a lifestyle change tend not to readjust their existing account balance: they tend to

allocate new contributions to a different asset class but leave whatever they already have in their GIC fund, as an example. The risk here is that they will not end up with the fruits of the asset allocation they thought they had.

Some employees will remain unconvinced of the value of asset allocation. They might be children of Depression-era parents, older workers with political objections or simply those with investment "war stories," their own or Uncle Bob's. Whatever the reason, Conseco's Dunlap advises "don't fight it." Since participants do not need to become Wall Street moguls, why push them into an asset mix that might cause sleepless nights?

Education consultants caution against forcing the issue of assuming more risk. If a person's goals indicate he or she needs to assume more risk than they want to, they must be prepared to save more. Tell them, "Don't assume more risk if you're not comfortable. But somehow you're going to have to accumulate the money."

COMPANY STOCK: A THORNY ISSUE

In a well-diversified portfolio, company stock does not necessarily carry a higher risk than any other option. But in reality, many 401(k) investors are invested too heavily in company stock and are extremely vulnerable as a result. Access Research, Inc. found that 23% of 401(k) assets are invested in employer stock.[15] This is an alarmingly high allocation, consultants say, and a difficult subject to address because it is so politically charged.

Having substantial allocations in company stock is often the result of working at a company that provides its 401(k) match in that form, sometimes in addition to an Employee Stock Ownership Plan (ESOP). Although many of these are stable, blue-chip, companies whose stocks have performed consistently well, employees face a double threat if they are heavily invested in company stock: their salary is tied to the company's fate and so is much of their retirement savings. Employees suffer if they lose their jobs, if the stock price declines or if the dividend is cut. Any of these events jeopardizes participants' retirement assets. Hefty company stock allocations in a 401(k) portfolio clearly violate sound diversification principles, yet for some 401(k) participants, company stock is their only equity investment.

This risk compounds when the equity allocation imbalance it creates remains uncorrected: if, at age 35, a participant had 50% of his or her 401(k) assets in company stock and the other 50% in GICs and left this allocation unadjusted, by the time he or she reaches age 65, the allocation would be closer to 70% company stock/ 30% fixed-income.

---

[15] "The Smart 401(k)," *Business Week*, July 3, 1995.

A disturbingly large number of 401(k) investors have this very allocation problem. "I'm very surprised the government hasn't set a limit to company stock, like the 10% limit it sets on the DB side," says one well-known pensions consultant.

How do education providers deal with this difficult subject? Corporate counsel often advise 401(k) administrators and treasury staff to steer clear of any talk regarding company stock in education programs. As a result, most consultants say they would not mention this issue specifically; they try to get the message across through teaching about diversification and asset allocation.

One consultant warns his clients that it's not in their best interest to have high levels of company stock in participants' 401(k) portfolios, if only because of possible future liability. Instead, he encourages clients to increase plan participation and persuade employees to raise contribution levels. In that case, even as employees diversify out of company stock, the total amount might easily remain level, since the decrease in the amount held by each participant would be offset by the number of new participants in the plan.

A few plan sponsors have preempted this problem by requesting permission from senior management to caution employees about company stock allocation. Schwanbeck of Times Mirror convinced his senior management to switch the company match from company stock to cash. Nat Duffield, Director of Trust Investments at Halliburton, says "we de-emphasize company stock" in the DC plan. "We tell them it's a lot riskier with only one stock and there are ways to own Halliburton stock outside the plan. It's enough of a risk that they could lose their job."

FIGHT THE URGE TO TIME THE MARKET

Once employees master basic concepts like risk/return, asset allocation and diversification, they should have a basis for understanding the dangers of market timing. It doesn't hurt for plan sponsor to underscore these dangers.

To illustrate the importance of staying the course, one consultant shows how three different people, each of whom started out in 1990 (the year the market plunged nearly 15% in three months) with $20,000 in their 401(k), ended up by 1993.

 Pamela, who shifted her money from the stable value fund to the stock market when stocks were hot in 1990, panicked when the market dropped and shifted back to stable value. After six months she moved back into stocks. Her account : $24,948.

 Jim, who kept his money throughout that period in the plan's stable value fund, ended 1993 with $25,869.

 Robert, who put his contributions in stocks all along, didn't change his allocation and didn't panic when the market dropped. He ended up the winner, with $29,960.

For the novice 401(k) investor, the moral to that story is clear. But how can you get the message across to more experienced, self-confident employees, particularly those who think of themselves as savvy stock-pickers? Simply warning against market timing won't work. Hewitt's Veeneman, for example, got a negative reaction to his cautionary reminder that if you try to time the market, you might "get your clocks cleaned." Now he says "you can pick and switch, or pick and stick; just make sure you do a good job of analyzing which approach works for you." He even gives participants a benchmark to use, choosing from among the lifestyle funds their employer may offer.

Ayco's Pape goes even further. After reminding participants that even gurus like Warren Buffet and Peter Lynch can't time the market, he dares participants "If you really believe you're good enough to make a fortune as a broker, go work for Smith Barney. If not, you're kidding yourself that you can be a successful market-timer."

WHEN CHOOSING

A PROVIDER FOR YOUR 01(k), DEFINED BENEFIT,

OR YOUR

40 3 (b)

PROGRAM,

THERE ARE 2 WAYS TO GO:

WITH A PROVIDER THAT DOES A LITTLE OR A LOT

OF EVERYTHING OR

A PARTNER WHO DOES 1 THING AND DOES IT…

VERY WELL INDEED.

Today, we manage over $8 billion in retirement plan assets ~ providing investment and recordkeeping services and helping over 300,000 participants save and invest wisely for retirement. And that's all we do. To see what such single-minded attention might mean for your organization's retirement program, *call* Chris Cumming, Vice President, at 1-800-770-6797.

DIVERSIFIED INVESTMENT ADVISORS

Partners in Retirement Solutions

PART
SIX

THE BIG PICTURE:
MAPPING YOUR STRATEGY

401(K) EDUCATION WITHIN A TOTAL
FINANCIAL PLANNING CONTEXT

In the past, financial planning was a perk offered chiefly to senior executives. Now, more and more, companies are offering financial planning services to all employees, with 401(k) education as only one component of programs that include general retirement planning, buying a home, financing college and other major lifetime expenses. A big-picture strategy can help employees use their benefits more effectively, while companies build goodwill and stay competitive. Many companies find employees who are more secure about their future make more productive workers.

Among the most important aspects of financial planning is managing big consumer purchases: a car, house, child's college education. How participants manage cash flow for these purchases determines how much they can invest for retirement and what their risk tolerance will be. "If you finance these purchases properly, you won't need to rely on your 401(k) for anything other than retirement," what the 401(k) was designed for, says education consultant Albin. Among his clients, he claims, the percentage of employees taking out loans dropped 37% as a result of showing workshop participants they don't have to use their 401(k) to pay for those expenses.

Not everyone believes in a total financial planning approach, however. Financial planning is an expensive, time-consuming process. It's not really possible to offer it cost effectively for employees on a widespread basis, say consultants, many of whom are former financial planners themselves. Plan sponsors, like Conseco's Dunlap, feel they should "stick to the fundamentals." General financial planning sometimes goes beyond what makes sense for the overall program; whether to lease or buy a car may be relevant for the $60,000-a-year employee, but it's not important for those making $25,000 a year, the employees with whom Dunlap's more concerned.

But the move toward setting 401(k) education within the broader context of overall financial planning is in fact already evident in many education materials. PSEG's video discusses insurance benefits, survivor planning and personal savings. The company combines its message about where the company's benefits "leave off and where your responsibility begins," with the optimistic reminder that through ongoing planning, participants can achieve seemingly overwhelming goals. Many consultants feel that plan sponsors can, ultimately, teach participants investment planning basics so that they will be able to manage their financial obligations by themselves.

If, as many consultants point out, the next wave in education will be to pre-retirees, the total financial planning concept makes sense. When thinking about 401(k) investing, we often think that "at age 65 we fall off a cliff." The real time horizon for most employees, in fact, extends well beyond age 65; at current longevity rates, people are already living as much as 25% of their lives in retirement.

PSEG's Quinn says his company's seminar program began as retirement planning for employees 50 years of age and older. Employees liked the program but wished they'd gotten the information earlier. Though the program still attracts predominantly older employees, Quinn hopes to get the 25- and 30-year-olds to attend.

What Happens When Your Education Program Succeeds?

Should your core curriculum change? Even as participants become smarter 401(k) investors, the core curriculum should not change. Companies have a constant stream of new employees and participants and the message holds: "Remember the need to communicate and reinforce basic structure and fundamentals," observes Ruebeck of Eli Lilly.

What about a long-range strategy? First and foremost, be responsive to employees' needs. Solicit feedback; listen to the questions they're asking. Stress and reinforce core concepts and basic information. It is possible to address the interests of both the new and more seasoned participant through newsletters, articles in the company publication, multi-level materials and special workshops.

Can Every Company Afford To Educate Its Employees?

Education programs, especially workshops, are not beyond the reach of mid-size and smaller companies. Depending on employee levels and years of service, the cost can run from $25 to $300 a year per employee (although on average it is closer to $100), with $300 buying 18 hours of seminar time.

If these costs are too high, or if the plan cannot absorb them, employers can consider the "shared responsibility" concept: have participants bear some or all of the cost. Mobil asks employees to cover the first $25 of the workshop fee and then picks up the rest. Ayco, the company's education provider, claims that it's a good idea to require employees to bear some of the cost. Others agree: "If it's free, you don't value it as much." You can mitigate the sting, and even apply the same funding technique as the 401(k) plan itself, by having a few dollars a week deducted from participants' paychecks over several pay periods.

Some plan sponsors offer the "back-end loaded" approach: the company pays in full, but if a participant misses a class he or she must subsidize the cost of the fee as a penalty for the missed class. 404(c) regulations, however, may discourage plan sponsors from asking employees to contribute to the cost of educational workshops. Many believe that whether or not they will face future liability, the cost of funding education programs now is far less than any potential cost, either of employees' inadequately funded 401(k) accounts or their distant lawsuits. Education programs are an investment in the company's future plan sponsors are increasingly willing to make.

The retirement crisis Americans face is daunting; it cannot be overstated. Given the long-term uncertainties of Social Security and Medicare, the dangerous consequences of not being able to provide for oneself in retirement—multiplied by the millions of employees who do not yet understand how dire those consequences could be—threaten each of us individually and the collective economic future of America. 401(k) education—as much as possible, as early as possible—has become, unequivocally, corporate America's moral and social, as well as its business, responsibility.

401(k) Data from Contributing Plan Sponsors

ADVANCED MICRO DEVICES, based in Sunnyvale, CA, manufactures microprocessors and integrated circuits for telecommunications and networking applications. As of September 30, 1995 the company's 401(k) plan had assets totaling $180.3 million, with 83% participation. The maximum contribution rate for employees is 15%, with an estimated 10% contributing at that level. The company offers a 50% match on the first 3% of the employee's contribution. Participant assets were allocated as follows: 52% to the aggressive (equity) growth fund; 20% to the stable value fund; 18% to the balanced fund; 10% to the growth fund. Since 1991 when education efforts began, employees have shifted more than 32% of their total assets out of the stable value fund and into higher-risk funds, particularly the aggressive growth fund.

ASEA BROWN BOVERI, INC., the world's largest engineering company with U.S. headquarters in Norwalk, CT, had $767 million in 401(k) assets as of September 30, 1995, with 90% participation. Employees may contribute up to 16%; the company offers a 50% match on the first 6% of the employee contribution. Participant assets were allocated as follows: 50% among three domestic fixed-income funds; 43% among four U.S. equity funds and 7% to international equity funds (one of which is emerging markets). Since education efforts began, employee contributions have shifted to 60% equity/40% fixed-income from an earlier ratio of 40% equity/60% fixed-income, and almost 10% of participants have increased their contribution level.

BECHTEL, the global engineering and construction firm based in San Francisco, CA, had $2.5 billion in its 401(k) as of September 30, 1995, with 95% participation. The maximum allowable employee contribution is 15%, with 31% of participants contributing at that level. The company provides a dollar-for-dollar match up to 5% (88% of employees contribute 5% or more). Participant assets were allocated as follows: 79% to the global (balanced) fund and 6% to the money market fund;

9% to an S&P 500 index fund; 2% to an intermediate bond fund; 2% to an aggressive domestic equity fund; 2% to an international equity fund. The most important result of education has been the development of a company-wide, "long-term" investment attitude.

CONSECO, the Carmel, IN-based financial services company, had $67 million in 401(k) assets as of June 30, 1995, with 60% participation. 10% of participants contribute the maximum 15%. The company offers a 50% match of the first 4% of employee contributions. Participant assets were allocated as follows: 33% to an interest income fund (primarily GICs); 29% to an equity fund; 12% to a money market fund; 11% to the company stock fund; 9% to a corporate bond fund; 6% to a government securities fund. Since education was implemented in December 1994, participation increased 25%, the company stock allocation dropped 3% and allocation to the equity fund rose 5%.

DAYTON HUDSON CORPORATION, the national retail chain headquartered in Minneapolis, MN, had $1.1 billion in 401(k) assets as of September 30, 1995, with nearly 50% participation. The company provides a dollar-for-dollar match up to 5% of the employee contribution. The maximum employee contribution is 15%, with 2% of participants contributing at that rate. Participant assets were allocated as follows: 53% to the variable interest fund (containing GICs and other fixed-income instruments) and 22% to company stock; 16% to an S&P 500 index fund; 3% to a balanced fund; 3% to the international fund; 3% to a long-term equity growth fund.

DIGITAL EQUIPMENT CORPORATION, headquartered in Maynard, MA, manufactures computers and integrated information systems. The company initiated a 2% match in July 1995 and added investment options, including international and pre-mixed portfolios. As of July 1, 1995 401(k) plan assets totaled $866 million, with 65% participation. Participant assets were allocated as follows: 41% to the stable value fund; 41% to the plan's four stock funds; 16% to three pre-mixed funds (made up of the plan's six fund choices) and 2% to the bond fund. With the increase in plan offerings, assets have shifted out of the stable value fund and into the international and moderate and aggressive pre-mixed funds. The maximum employee contribution is 8% or 12%, depending on salary.

ELI LILLY & CO., a pharmaceutical company headquartered in Indianapolis, IN, had, as of September 30, 1995, total 401(k) plan assets of $1.8 billion, with more than 90% participation. Nearly 50% of participants contribute the annual maximum allowed by the IRS. The company offers a match between 50 cents and $1 per employee dollar, depending upon profitability. Aggregate asset allocation was 47.9% in company stock; 18.8% in the stable income fund; 12.5% in the aggressive stock fund; 12.3% in a diversified assets (global balanced) fund and 9% in its U.S. equity index fund.

HALLIBURTON COMPANY is a global energy, engineering and construction company based in Dallas, TX. As of October 31, 1995 its total defined contribution assets (including the 401(k), after-tax savings and profit-sharing plans) stood at nearly $3 billion, with participation at 63%. Aggregate asset allocation was as follows: 52.8% to the general investment fund, which contains diversified assets; 41.1% to the fixed-income fund; 3.7% to the equity investment fund and 2.4% to the company stock fund. 8% of participants contribute the 15% maximum allowed. The company matches 25% on the first 4% of employee contributions.

MOBIL CORPORATION is based in Fairfax, VA. As of September 30, 1995 401(k) plan assets totaled $1.9 billion, with 58% participation. Maximum employee contribution is 8% for Highly Compensated Employees (HCEs) and 13% for non-HCEs. 60% of HCEs contribute the maximum; 10% of non-HCEs contribute the maximum. The company provides a 6% match, regardless of whether the employee contributes to the plan, divided as follows: 4% to the ESOP and 2% to either common stock or cash [for take-home or contribution to the 401(k)]. Mobil offers 11 fund choices, with participant assets allocated as follows: 44.2% to company stock; 22.7% to a large-cap equity fund; 16.4% to a stable value fund; 5.7% to a money market fund; 2.9% to a global balanced fund; 1.9% to an equity growth fund; 1.8% to a growth and income (balanced) fund; 1.7% to an S&P 500 equity index fund; 1.1% to a U.S. government securities (mostly GNMA) fund; 1% to a global equity fund and 0.6% to an emerging markets fund. Before education was implemented, 67% of participant assets were invested in equities (41% company stock, 26% other). Two years later (August 1995), the total equity allocation had increased more than 6% (to 44% in company stock, 29% other).

MONTANA POWER COMPANY is a utility and diversified energy company based in Butte, MT. As of September 30, 1995 401(k) assets totaled $185 million, across four plans, with 91% total participation. 80% of participants contribute the maximum: 6% pre-tax and 10% after-tax. The company offers a scaled match: 60% for employees with up to 10 years service; 65% from 10 to 20 years and 70% for employees 20 years and over. Assets are allocated as follows: 31.6% for the fixed-rate income fund; 62.8% for the equity fund and 5.6% for the bond fund.

NESTLE USA, INC. is the diversified food products company headquartered in Glendale, CA. As of September 30, 1995 401(k) plan assets totaled $627 million, with 85% participation. Employees may contribute up to 15% of pay. The company matches $.50 on the dollar up to 6% of pay. Participant assets were allocated as follows: 40% to the stable investments fund; 27% to the balanced fund; 26% to a common stock fund; 4% to a small company stock fund and 3% to an international stock fund. These allocations include assets invested in four pre-set portfolios composed of the plan's five funds.

To know us is to know

ROGERSCASEY

DEFINED CONTRIBUTION
SERVICES GROUP

ONE PARKLANDS DRIVE DARIEN, CT 06820-1460

RogersCasey knows your world.
Since 1976, we have fused
knowledge of the Defined Contribution
marketplace with understanding of
the investment management field.
Today we are a source of
applied investment solutions.
Solutions for structuring a better plan.
For choosing the best options,
vendors, and managers.
For delivering more effective
participant services and education.

RogersCasey works for your world.
More than 100 plan sponsors,
who represent over $250 billion
in retirement assets, value our
knowledge and counsel.

Isn't it time you got to know us?

Call the Defined Contribution
Services Group at 203 656 5900.

your

world.

PUBLIC SERVICE ENTERPRISE GROUP is the Newark, NJ-based holding company of regional utilities. Its non-union 401(k) pension plan had $390 million in assets as of August 31, 1995, with 85% participation. Employees may contribute 25% of pay up to IRS limits. The company matches 50% of the first 6% of the employee contribution. Participant assets were allocated as follows: 59.2% to the GIC fund; 13.8% to the company stock fund; 11% to an S&P 500 fund; 5.4% to an aggressive stock fund; 2.8% to an international stock fund; 2.3% to a utility index fund; 2.3% to a balanced fund and 1.5% to a government bond fund. (1.8% is frozen in a now-defunct ESOP.) Since mid-1992 when education was introduced, the allocation to the company stock fund fell by 6.9% and by 6.2% to the GIC fund. In the same period, allocations to the aggressive stock fund grew by 3.4%, and to the S&P 500 fund by 2.7%.

THE TIMES MIRROR COMPANY, the international media company with U.S. headquarters in Los Angeles, CA, had $464.2 million in 401(k) assets as of June 30, 1995, with close to 80% participation. Non-HCEs can contribute up to 24% (between pre- and after-tax contributions); HCEs are allowed up to 8% in contributions. The company provides a match of 50% on the first 6% of the employee contribution, with a maximum of 3% or 6%. Participant assets were allocated as follows: 28.1% to an equity fund; 23.6% to the company stock fund; 23.8% to an income fund (bonds); 13.4% to a global equity fund; 11.1% to a balanced fund. Since their education program began in 1991, the income and company stock funds saw significant reductions in allocations.

U S West, the Baby Bell telecommunications company, serves 14 Western states from its base in Englewood, CO. As of September 30, 1995, 401(k) plan assets totaled $3.1 billion, with 90% participation. The company offers a match of 66⅔% or 83⅓% of the first 6% contributed, depending on company division. Aggregate asset allocation was: 54% in company stock; 17% in the interest income fund (which contains GICs and other instruments); 12% in the S&P 500 index fund; 9% in the U.S. balanced fund; 4% in the international stock fund and 2% in the global fund (stocks and bonds). The remaining 2% is in loans. After education programs were implemented, the employee contributions to the equity funds grew by 4% and participation rose 10 percentage points to 90%.

XEROX CORPORATION, based in Stamford, CT, is the international manufacturer and marketer of document processing equipment. As of September 30, 1995 401(k) assets totaled $1.8 billion, with close to 58% participation. Participant assets were allocated as follows: 39% to an income fund, consisting chiefly of GICs and bonds; 34% to a balanced fund containing large and small-cap equities, bonds, venture capital, real estate and other asset classes, each of which is managed in separate accounts by Xerox's defined benefit managers; 8% to the company stock fund; 7% to the international stock fund; 6% to the U.S. stock fund and 6% to the small company stock fund. HCEs may contribute up to 10% of pre-tax income and 1% of after-tax income; non-HCEs are permitted to contribute 18% of pre-tax income. Xerox discontinued the company match in 1990 when its overall pension and saving plan benefit program was revamped.

RESOURCE GUIDE

THE INVESTORS PRESS RESOURCE GUIDE IS A SERIES OF SPECIAL SECTIONS INTENDED TO ENHANCE THE EDUCATIONAL VALUE OF THIS BOOK AND EXTEND ITS USEFULNESS AS A REFERENCE TOOL AND RESOURCE.

➤ UNDERWRITER PROFILES

➤ ANNOTATED BIBLIOGRAPHY

➤ GLOSSARY OF INVESTMENT RISKS

➤ AUTHORS' BIOGRAPHIES

UNDERWRITER PROFILES

Allmerica Financial Institutional Services

440 Lincoln Street, Worcester, MA 01653

Key Contacts: 508-853-AFIS
Jeffrey Lagarce, *Senior Vice President*
Kathleen Klein, *Senior Vice President*

Organization: Allmerica Financial Institutional Services is a subsidiary of First Allmerica Financial Life Insurance Company. For over 150 years, the Allmerica Financial family of companies has provided insurance protection and financial security to its clients. With over 50 years in the retirement industry, more than 1,000 clients, and $4 billion in institutional assets under management, AFIS's experience and resources provide a plan that maximizes plan participation and employee contributions and minimizes plan sponsor involvement.

AFIS offers a wide range of retirement and benefit products and asset management services, including:
- annuities and insurance
- retirement and employee benefit plans
- strategic and tactical distribution support
- asset management and trust services

Retirement programs: AFIS offers a full range of retirement programs, including Allmerica Choice, a complete 401(k) plan. Choice reduces the plan sponsor's administrative and fiduciary burdens by emphasizing employee education, offering a variety of investment options and providing high-level service for employers and employees.

Our employee education program includes an interactive multimedia enrollment presentation, workbooks and asset allocation worksheets and complete investment option information.

The Choice investment options are managed by some of the country's leading institutional money managers, including Nicholas-Applegate Capital Management and Fidelity Investments. An independent evaluation committee monitors the performance and practices of the money managers to insure performance that is comparable to or better than industry benchmarks.

AFIS is committed to its clients: we are determined to design the right solutions through a consultative approach, to provide superior customer service and to offer a complete package of bundled services tailored to their needs.

American Express Financial Advisors Inc.

P.O. Box 489, Minneapolis, MN 55440-0489

Key Contacts:
American Express
Institutional Services   1-800-437-0600
(*A division of American Express Financial Advisors Inc.*)
Robert Rudell, *President*   (612) 671-2565
Ward Armstrong, *Sr. Vice President*   (612) 671-1915

Year Founded: 1894

Assets Under Management:
Total American Express Financial Advisors Inc.
    Clients: 1.9M   Assets: $124B
American Express Institutional Services
    Clients: 852**   Assets: $10B*
    Custodial Assets: $68.7B*

 * As of 10/31/95; asset figures for American Express
    Trust Company
** Corporate/institutional clients

Special Areas of Expertise: American Express Institutional Services, a division of American Express Financial Advisors Inc., along with American Express Trust Company, offers the complete defined contribution/401(k) plan outsourcing solution—from investments, trust and recordkeeping to employee education. American Express Financial Advisors offers a range of mutual fund products to both institutional and retail clients, all developed and managed to represent the various risk/return steps on the investment spectrum. American Express Trust Company provides collective funds specifically designed for qualified plans and managed in compliance with ERISA. American Express Trust Company also provides separate stable capital account management services. Access to outside money management is available to qualified plan investors through the SmartPartners^{SM} alliance.

Investment Approach: For all our disciplines, our investment philosophy is consistent with our 102-year history. We believe our approach is well suited to the needs of retirement plan sponsors and participants. By consistently applying the disciplined, hands-on management skills acquired through more than 50 years in fund management, American Express Financial Advisors seeks to manage investments without exposing plan participants to more near-term volatility than is necessary to seek to achieve the investment objective.

CIGNA Retirement & Investment Services

350 Church Street, Hartford, CT 06103
Phone: 800-997-6633 • Fax 203-725-2052

Key Contacts:
Douglas E. Klinger, *Senior Vice President Marketing & Business Development*
Frederick C. Castellani, *Senior Vice President Sales*

Assets Under Management:

Discretionary Assets	$65 Billion
Tax-Exempt Assets	$37 Billion
401(k) Assets	$18 Billion

Special Areas of Expertise:
CIGNA, with over 70 years of institutional investment management and retirement plan experience, is one of the nation's leading providers of retirement plan services. With 24 dedicated regional offices nationwide, CIGNA manages retirement assets for more than 5,000 organizations, including public and private corporations, unions, associations and government entities. We offer a full range of bundled and unbundled services, a flexible, state-of-the-art relational database daily recordkeeping system and comprehensive investment options through our Multi-Manager Matrix of nationally recognized investment managers.

Investment Approach:
CIGNA Retirement & Investment Services offers single-source accessibility to a comprehensive array of top-performing investment products from CIGNA and other major mutual fund complexes and independent money managers. The foundation of our approach is our rigorous screening, selection and performance measurement process designed to provide the benefit of advance due diligence to plan sponsors. Our key objective is to provide access to consistently superior investment strategies across all major asset classes.

Retirement and investment products are provided by subsidiaries of CIGNA Corporation, including CIGNA Investments, Inc. and Connecticut General Life Insurance Company.

Diversified Investment Advisors

Four Manhattanville Road, Purchase, NY 10577
Phone 800-770-6797 • Fax 914-697-3743

Key Contact:
James G. Russell, *VP– Investment Marketing*

The Firm:
Diversified offers comprehensive programs of high-quality investments and administrative services to Defined Benefit, Defined Contribution and Not-for-Profit plan sponsors. Diversified forms a partnership with its clients to provide exceptional investment management, plan design, participant communication programs, recordkeeping services and technical guidance.

Total Retirement Assets Under Management:
$8 Billion

Discretionary Assets Under Management:
$1 Billion

Investment Philosophy:
Diversified's investment approach is founded on four fundamental principles:
• Performance is overwhelmingly influenced by strategic asset allocation.
• Asset allocation requires a broad array of funds representing major asset classes.
• Efficient investing through asset allocation demands specialized expertise in managing assets to strict investment objectives. Diversified achieves this through the selection of highly accomplished, independent investment managers.
• Continuous monitoring of each manager is essential to assure strict adherence to the investment objective of each asset class.

Special Qualified Plan Features:
• Customized asset allocation advisory service.
• Access to a full spectrum of investment options, managed by 17 independent money management firms utilizing 34 portfolio managers.
• Diversified's 401(k) Service Guarantee.
• Diversified's 403(b) "Audit Proof" Program
• Access to a full range of self-directed investment options including individual stocks and bonds as well as over 800 mutual funds through Charles Schwab & Co. Inc.

Fidelity Investments®

82 Devonshire Street, Boston, MA 02109

Key Contacts:

Fidelity Institutional Retirement Services Company

Robert Reynolds, *President*	508-787-8787
Peter Smail, *Senior Vice President*	508-787-8090

Fidelity Management Trust Company

Denis M. McCarthy

President & CEO	617-563-7238
Edward E. Madden, *Vice Chairman*	617-563-6144

Year Founded: 1946

Total Assets :

	NUMBER OF CLIENTS	ASSETS (*in millions*)
Total Retirement Services Company	6,100	$95 Billion*
Total Management Trust Company	220	$32 Billion**

*as of 9/30/95 **as of 11/30/95

Special Areas of Expertise: Fidelity Institutional Retirement Services Company (FIRSCO) is a leading provider of retirement benefit plan services. FIRSCO offers a full ensemble of participant and plan sponsor support services that give our clients the ability to outsource all benefit plan administration with a single, integrated service provider. Fidelity Management Trust Company provides investment management services for institutional clients worldwide through separate account management and commingled pools. The firm offers a wide range of investment disciplines, each focusing on a particular market segment or set of investment characteristics.

Investment Approach: For all our disciplines, our investment philosophy is consistent with Fidelity's 50-year history.

Fundamental Research: We base our decision-making on in-depth knowledge of companies and credits.

Adherence to Investment Disciplines: A consistent, well thought-out investment discipline governs each portfolio's objectives, investment universe, buy and sell disciplines, desired characteristics and expected performance pattern.

Fully Invested Portfolios: Fidelity does not engage in market timing.

Portfolio Managers Have Responsibility and Accountability: Within their disciplines, portfolio managers have broad investment latitude and unlimited access to resources, and they are strictly accountable for performance.

Fleet Investment Advisors

100 Westminster Street, Providence, RI 02903

Key Contacts:

Marshall Raucci, Jr.

Executive Vice President	401-278-3318

Year Founded: 1791

The Company:

Fleet Financial Group is one of the nation's oldest and largest financial services and banking institutions with over $80 billion in assets and more than 1,200 offices nationwide. Fleet Investment Advisors, a subsidiary of Fleet Financial Group, offers specialized services to corporations and consumers, including investment management, retirement plan administration and trust services.

Services:

Fleet Investment Advisors Inc. has successfully managed 401(k) plans since these plans were first authorized by the I.R.S. in the early 1980s. Over the years, we've invested heavily in people and state-of-the-art systems, gaining the expertise and strength that comes only with experience. Fleet Investment Advisors, through our RETIREMENT PLUS SM program, is a leading single-source provider of full-service 401(k) and other defined contribution plan services, including:

- On-site and in-person employee education and enrollment services
- Ongoing employee education and communication programs
- A comprehensive array of professionally managed investment options, including the Galaxy Family of mutual funds and other selected mutual fund families
- "True" daily transaction processing and valuation of participant accounts
- In-depth evaluation of client plan design and documents
- Reliable delivery of administration and ongoing account service.

Special Areas of Expertise:

Fleet Investment Advisors offers national caliber investment management, administrative services and comprehensive employee education.

MetLife

One Madison Ave., New York, NY 10010

Key Contacts:

Nicholas Latrenta, *Vice President*		212-578-3761
Gary Lineberry, *Vice President*		212-578-3181
Felix Schirripa, *Vice President*		212-578-6492

Total tax-exempt assets under management from all sources: $80.5 Billion

Wholly Owned Investment Management Subsidiaries:

State Street Research & Management Company actively manages equity and fixed-income assets for individual and institutional separate accounts and mutual funds. MetLife Investment Management Corporation (MIMCO) provides active fixed-income management of diversified, mortgage-backed, asset-backed, private placement, and duration-constrained portfolios for individual and commingled separate accounts. GFM International Investors, Ltd., London, specializes in active non-U.S equity and fixed-income management of separate account and mutual fund products.

Number of Clients (all sources):

Corporate Funds	1,345
Public Funds	120
Unions (Taft-Hartley)	90
Foundations & Endowments	8

as of 6/30/95

Investment Approaches:

State Street Research draws upon specialized internal research and bottom-up equity analysis. A top-down fixed-income philosophy utilizes interest rate forecasting, yield curve analysis and duration constraints. MIMCO achieves incremental return to fixed-income portfolios through duration management, sector weighting, issue selection, yield curve analysis and interest rate anticipation, with emphasis on credit and quantitative research. GFM's active management strategy includes country allocation, currency weighting and issue selection. In the firm's core macroeconomic view, equity selections are based upon fundamental valuation methods, while fixed-income issues are selected through the variation of interest rate exposure, yield curve analysis and maturity structure.

NationsBank

100 North Tryon Street, Charlotte, NC 28255

Key Contact:

Pamela J. Hubby, *SVP*
Retirement Services Sales   404-607-4999

The Company: NationsBank Corporation, the parent company of NationsBank, N.A. ("NationsBank"), is currently the third largest bank holding company in the U.S. With over 60,000 professionals in 4,000 offices, NationsBank and its banking affiliates serve more than 5.2 million retail and 550,000 business customers in all aspects of financial services.

Retirement Services: A wide array of retirement plans is available through NationsBank, including 401(k) plans providing unique solutions to customer needs. In addition to investment management, administrative, document and trustee services, NationsBank provides plan sponsors with a comprehensive communications program that helps participants understand the risks of long-term investing and how to determine optimal risk/reward profiles based on their individual needs. NationsBank currently administers over $110 billion in institutional assets for over 3,500 companies nationwide.

Investment Expertise: Since 1874, NationsBank and its predecessors have provided prudent investment management and trust services to individuals, institutions, foundations and endowments. The mutual fund family advised by NationsBank ranks among the top five bank advised mutual funds based on asset size and is the 28th largest fund complex out of 615 bank- and nonbank-affiliated fund families. Forty-three mutual fund portfolios total over $17 billion in assets under management.

Plan Sponsor and Participant Services:

NationsBank provides retirement plan services designed to simplify the role of the plan sponsor and encourage a high level of participation among employees. Our expertise in sponsor and participant services includes:

- Plan enrollment documentation and services
- Accurate recordkeeping, maintenance and administrative services
- Timely statements and reporting procedures
- Customized employee communications
- Educational materials
- Enrollment and educational seminars.

Neuberger & Berman Management Inc.
605 Third Avenue, New York, NY 10158

Key Contacts:
N&B Management Institutional Services
Peter Sundman, *National Director*   212-476-8924
Susan Walsh, *Assistant Vice President*
Institutional Services   212-476-8928

Year Founded:
Neuberger & Berman   1939
Neuberger & Berman Management Inc.   1970

Assets Under Management:
Total Neuberger & Berman $ 37.6 Billion
N&B Management Mutual Funds $ 11.2 Billion
N&B Pension
   Endowment/Institutional $ 15.6 Billion
N&B High Net Worth $ 10.8 Billion

About Our Firm:
Neuberger & Berman Management Inc. is the investment manager, administrator and distributor of a family of equity and fixed-income no-load mutual funds, including funds used in insurance company products.

Focus On 401(k)s:
Our Institutional Department is dedicated to servicing plan sponsors in the 401(k) and defined contribution markets. In addition to providing investment options for qualified plans, Neuberger & Berman Management also provides employee education, enrollment meetings and plan sponsor support.

Investment Approach:
Each of our equity funds follow one of two basic investment approaches: value or growth. Most of our equity fund portfolio managers pursue the value approach, believing that, over time, undervalued securities are most likely to appreciate in price and be subject to less risk of price decline than securities whose market prices have already reached their perceived economic value. With our fixed-income funds, we follow a similarly limited-risk approach, seeking high total returns consistent with minimal risk to capital.

NYL Benefit Services Company, Inc.
A New York Life Company
846 University Avenue, Norwood, MA 02062-2641

Key Contacts:
NYL Benefit Services Company:
Joel M. Disend, President   617-440-2000
Jane Wallace, *Executive Assistant*   800-586-1413
Mike Anderson, *Vice President*
Eastern Region   703-312-5113
Steve Patterson, *Vice President*
Central Region   312-781-0100
Chris M. Blair, *Vice President*
Western Region   415-956-1155

Year Founded:
NYL Benefit Services Company
(formerly ADQ, Inc.)   1970
New York Life   1845

Assets Under Management*:
New York Life Insurance Company and Affiliates
Consolidated Assets $92.4 Billion*
* as of 9/30/95

Special Areas of Expertise:
NYL Benefit Services provides a complete range of retirement plan, benefit consulting and administration services, including a bundled 401(k) program—401(k) Complete[SM]. A full spectrum of mutual funds is available through NYLIFE Securities Inc., member NASD, including MainStay Institutional Funds, Inc. Guaranteed products, including the Pooled Stable Value Account, as well as Separate Accounts, are offered by triple-A rated[**] New York Life Insurance Company.

[**] Independent services rate companies on a number of factors, including financial strength and claims-paying ability. Several of the leading services gave New York Life their highest rating—Moody's Investors Service: Aaa, based on financial strength; Standard & Poor's and Duff & Phelps Corporation: AAA for claims-paying ability; and A.M. Best Company, Inc.: A++ (Superior) for financial strength. These ratings apply to New York Life Insurance Company, not to any investment products offered by the company.

Prudential Defined Contribution Services (Pru-DC)

30 Scranton Office Park, Moosic, PA 18507

Key Contact Information:

Robert E. Lee, *Vice President*
Marketing & Communications Group   717-341-6005

History:

Founded in 1875, The Prudential has been a manager of pension assets since 1928. In 1963, The Prudential began providing investment management, record-keeping and educational communication services to defined contribution plans. In 1992, Pru-DC, an independent business unit, was established to provide full-service defined contribution administration to the mid-sized market.

Total Assets Under Management From All Prudential Sources (The Prudential):

$297 Billion

as of 12/31/94

Defined Contribution Assets: $33 Billion

as of 9/30/95

Reporting of Valuation: Daily

Minimum Account Size: $1 Million

Special Areas of Expertise:

Pru-DC is dedicated to providing institutional investment management, recordkeeping and investment education services. The diversity of investment choice available at Pru-DC—mutual funds, separate accounts and conservative stable-value options managed over the long-term—is attractive to any investor. We offer some of the industry's most experienced investment professionals, recognized for their specialized investment expertise. Our advanced recordkeeping system integrates image processing, a voice response system and daily valuation to ensure responsive, efficient service. We also provide a specialized team of professionals dedicated to implement new plans to ensure a smooth transition to Pru-DC. Award-winning investment education materials round out our services to give employees comprehensive, flexible and effective investment communications.

Rogers, Casey & Associates, Inc.

One Parklands Drive, Darien, CT 06820
Phone 203-656-5900 • Fax 203-656-2233

Key Contacts:

Gregg A. Robinson
Director, Marketing   203-656-5950

Kenneth G. Rogers
Managing Dir., Marketing   203-656-5940

Year Founded: 1976; employee-owned

Business Mission: RogersCasey is a research-based global investment services firm committed to delivering value-added consultative services and products that enable institutional investors to exceed their goals in complex and fast-changing market environments.

Client Service: RogersCasey's expertise is in the design, implementation and monitoring of investment programs. A team approach allows clients to access information and issue-solving capabilities firmwide. Each client is assigned a relationship team with accountability for all day-to-day activities. In addition, research specialists have responsibility for coverage of specific asset classes. These specialists are called upon as needed to assist with client assignments.

Assets Represented by Client Category*:

	NUMBER OF CLIENTS	ASSETS (in millions)
Corporate	65	$175
Public	12	100
Foundations & Endowments	6	5
Other	20	5

*As of 9/30/95

Services:

Investment Consulting:
    Defined benefit pension, Endowment, Foundation, Insurance, Hospital, etc.
Defined Contribution:
    Investments, administration and education
Alternative Investments:
    Private markets
Strategic Investments:
    Customized multi-manager programs.

Stanwich Benefits Group, Inc.
Actuarial & Recordkeeping Services
The Centre at Purchase
3 Manhattanville Road, Purchase, NY 10577
Phone 914-253-0700 • Fax 914-253-0701

Key contacts:
Robert A. Goldstein, *President*
Steven J. Levine, *Senior Vice President*

The Company: Stanwich specializes in the custom recordkeeping and actuarial services for defined contribution, defined benefit and welfare plans you would expect to receive from a consulting firm. Some recordkeeping programs use a uniform approach; Stanwich recognizes the unique needs of each employee and plan sponsor. The Stanwich automated and live operator call center provide a custom-designed outsourcing service. Our actuaries and consultants provide the expertise to address all compliance and design issues.

Stanwich addresses all the needs: We process hundreds of thousands of participant accounts daily. Many plans require a customized approach with multiple fund family transactions, GICs or employer stock. We support companies that require services to be coordinated among multiple plans and compliance issues to be monitored across controlled groups.

Stanwich Professionals: Our professional education requirements result in the highest professional credentials for our people. Most of our managers hold FSPA, EA, CPC, MAAA and CEBS designations and all managers have more than 10 years' experience in their field.

Stanwich meets the technical needs. Our expertise supports the plan and sponsor needs for plan qualification under IRC 401(a). We monitor the deductibility of plan contributions under IRC §404, the coverage requirements under §410(b), the nondiscrimination requirements under §401(a)(4), IRC §401(k) and §401(m), and the limitation under IRC §415. Our call center can support the participant inqiry and distribution of information under ERISA §404(c).

Stanwich is the answer to the plan that needs a consulting firm's capabilities, high-level professional expertise, complete live call center outsourcing of plan functions and a custom approach to design and administration.

Strong Funds
Strong Capital Management
One Hundred Heritage Reserve, P.O. Box 2936
Milwaukee, WI 53201
Phone: 800-338-9699 • Fax: 414-359-3888

Key Contacts:
Rochelle Lamm Wallach, *President*
Strong Advisory Services

The Company: Founded in 1974, Strong Capital Management manages more than $15 billion for over 500,000 individuals and institutions. Strong's nationally recognized mutual funds are 100% no-load. Strong Retirement Plan Services provides a full range of retirement plan services—investment management, daily valuation recordkeeping, plan administration/compliance, and participant education and communications—all with an important distinction. At Strong, we understand that investment performance alone is not enough: you and your employees deserve much more—competence, attention to detail and a can-do approach. In short, outstanding service in everything we do.

Retirement Plan Services:
- Open Architecture investment selection, including Strong Mutual Funds, other well-known mutual funds, a stable value fund and company stock.
- State-of-the-Art Daily Valuation recordkeeping.
- Complete Enrollment Materials and On-site Educational Workshops delivered by experienced educators and communication specialists.
- Easy-to-Read Participant Statements, including asset allocation models, and 24-hour access to Strong's Automated Telephone Information System.
- Partnership Not Salesmanship. A team of expert retirement plan specialists works with you throughout the life of your plan. Our account managers are attorneys, CPAs or hold graduate business degrees.

Investment Disciplines:

Domestic Equity	International Equity
Domestic Fixed-Income	Cash Management
International Fixed-Income	

Expert plan administration, state-of-the-art recordkeeping, comprehensive employee communications and flexible investment options—all in a one source approach. That's the Strong Advantage.

T. Rowe Price Associates, Inc.
100 East Pratt Street
Baltimore, MD 21202

Key Contacts:
T. Rowe Price Retirement Plan Services, Inc.
(A subsidiary of T. Rowe Price Associates, Inc.)

Charles E. Vieth, *President*	410-547-5763
John R. Rockwell, *SVP, Sales*	410-547-2077

Year Founded: 1937

TRPA Assets Under Management: $72 Billion
(as of 9/30/95)

Special Areas of Expertise:
T. Rowe Price Associates offers a wide range of mutual funds and investment management services to institutional and retail clients. Retirement Plan Services is the subsidiary dedicated to meeting the needs of the defined contribution market. A pioneer in offering mutual funds as retirement options, T. Rowe Price provides investments, plan sponsor services, and participant services that can be tailored to meet a client's specific needs.

Investment Approach:
T. Rowe Price's investment approach is based on fundamental research and strict adherence to fund objectives. We seek consistent, strong, risk-adjusted performance.

Plan Sponsor Services:
T. Rowe Price provides plan sponsors with a complete array of recordkeeping and plan-related services. Clients benefit from more than a decade of experience in providing innovative solutions.

Participant Services:
T. Rowe Price has for years been at the forefront of investor education. We are committed to helping participants understand how to plan and invest to achieve a financially secure retirement.

Index to Underwriters

ANNOTATED BIBLIOGRAPHY

RECOMMENDATIONS FROM THE AUTHORS AND INVESTORS PRESS

A hands-down favorite:
One Up on Wall Street, by Peter Lynch (New York: Simon & Schuster, 1989; Penguin 1990), an engaging volume of basic, bottom-up (and time-tested) principles of investing, illustrated through personal anecdotes from the legendary former manager of Fidelity's Magellan Fund. Lynch's modesty and even-handed treatment of his failures, along with his successes, make for interesting and edifying reading.

Atlas of Economic Indicators, by W. Stansbury Carnes and Stephen D. Slifer (New York: HarperCollins, 1991), is a handy guide that helps readers understand the impact of the stream of economic data released daily; includes plenty of graphs.

Evaluating Training Programs: The Four Levels, by D. Kirkpatrick (San Francisco: Berrett-Koehler, 1994) is a "how-to" for those who plan, implement and evaluate training programs. In financial education, results are not usually measured; this book provides a practical and proven model for increasing the effectiveness of education by evaluating its results.

Figuring Things Out: A Trainer's Guide to Needs and Task Analysis, by R. Zemke and T. Kramlinger (Reading, MA: Addison-Wesley, 1982) is a handy catalog of tactics, techniques and procedures designed to help you conduct effective organizational studies and determine training needs. This book helps readers determine your company's investment education goals and provides ways to measure the success of your education programs.

Helping Employees Achieve Retirement Security: A Guide for 401(k) Administrators, by R. Theodore Benna, "father of the 401(k)" and president of the national 401(k) Association (Washington Depot, CT: Investors Press, 1995), offers clear and concise explanations of plan administration issues, common problems and solutions, as well as more than 60 pages of answers to 401(k) participants' most often asked questions. A companion volume, **Building Your Nest Egg With Your 401(k): A Guide To Help You Achieve Retirement Security,** by Lynn Brenner (Washington Depot, CT: Investors Press, 1995), is written specifically for plan participants and eligible enrollees and teaches them the basics of 401(k) investing; it, too, features an in-depth Q&A section.

Keys to Investing in Mutual Funds, by Warren Boroson (Hauppauge, NY: Barron's Educational Series, 1989), another from *Barron's* useful *Keys to* financial series; and **Guide to Mutual Funds**, by Kurt Brouwer (New York: John Wiley & Sons, 1990), are both particularly popular.

Manage Your 401(k) with Confidence, by Steven Winkler, CFP (Livonia, MI: Capital Consulting Group) is a basic handbook for plan participants that explains why their plan is important, gives plain-English investment basics and offers help to design a retirement investment game plan. Available through the author/publisher: 17197 N. Laurel Park Drive, Suite 135, Livonia, Michigan 48152.

The New Century Family Money Book, by Jonathan Pond (New York: Doubleday, 1994). Pond is a financial planner and writer who also conducts 401(k) educational seminars.

Personal Finance for Dummies, by Eric Tyson (Foster City, CA: IDG Books Worldwide, Inc., 1994), another hot seller in the "For Dummies" series and a non-intimidating primer that covers everything from mutual funds and retirement planning to credit cards, spending reduction and insurance.

The Retirement Myth, by Craig S. Karpel (New York: HarperCollins, 1995). The author, a journalist trained in economics, joins the growing number of analysts who believe the American notion of retirement is an anomaly—a reality only for the World War II generation. In this provocative and controversial book he argues that the costs of retirement are draining America: Social Security is shrinking, defined contribution plans are rapidly replacing defined benefit plans and our GNP and housing stock are declining. Karpel predicts early retirement will disappear and the retirement age will be postponed for everyone. The news isn't completely dreary, however: later retirement has its economic and social pluses.

Stocks, Bonds, Bills and Inflation: The Past and the Future, by Roger G. Ibbotson and Rex A. Sinquefield (Chicago: Ibbotson Associates). Published annually, this "bible" of returns and risks is a useful bookshelf reference. Its precise charts and graphs are used as standard illustrations in most employee communications and education materials.

Stocks for the Long Run, by Jeremy J. Siegel (Burr Ridge, IL: Irwin Professional Publishing, 1994). Siegel, a highly regarded professor of finance at the University of Pennsylvania's Wharton School of Business, shows why long-term investors should invest in stocks; he generates data going as far back as the 1800s.

Sylvia Porter's New Money Book for the 80s, (New York: Avon Books, 1979); **Sylvia Porter's Your Financial Security** (New York: Avon Books, 1989); and **Sylvia Porter's Your Finances in the 90s** (New York: Prentice-Hall, 1990); also **Making the Most of Your Money: Smart Ways to Create Wealth and Plan Your Finances in the 1990s** by Jane Bryant Quinn (New York: Simon & Schuster, 1991). Quinn, the consumer advocate of personal finance, writes a weekly column for *Newsweek*.

Training for Impact: How to Link Training to Business Needs and Measure the Results, by D. Robinson and J. Robinson (San Francisco: Jossey-Bass, 1989) is a straightforward 12-step approach plan administrators can use to link their financial education programs directly to their company's needs, problems and opportunities. It explains how to develop a collaborative "client-consultant" relationship with line managers that will ensure their support, and includes hands-on tools to help document the success of education efforts.

Understanding and Facilitating Adult Learning, by S. Brookfield (San Francisco: Jossey-Bass, 1986). Despite the increasing number of adults enrolling in education and training programs, theories, teaching methods, program designs and instructional approaches have not kept pace with changing adult needs. This book analyzes current approaches to adult learning, presents a comprehensive review of how adults learn and proposes ways to develop more creative, up-to-date adult education programs.

The Wall Street Journal Guide to Money & Investing, by Kenneth Morris (New York: Simon & Schuster, 1994), covers all the basics: stocks, bonds, mutual funds, futures and money itself; and **The Wall Street Journal Guide to Understanding Personal Finance,** by Kenneth Morris (New York: Simon & Schuster, 1995); both receive high marks from a number of sources.

The Wealthy Barber, by David Chilton (Rocklin, CA: Prima Publishing, 1991), is a best-selling novel inspired by the TV series "Cheers" in which the protagonist, a barber, educates his customers about financial and retirement planning. Humorous and entertaining, it is popular among plan sponsors in the know because it gets the message across. A two-part educational video based on the book is available by calling 313-876-8161.

Your 401(k) Plan: How and Where to Invest, by Mark L. Schwanbeck (Burr Ridge, IL: Irwin Professional Publishing, 1994). Schwanbeck explores the basics of the 401(k) plan, reviews common investment choices, discusses asset allocation and guides the novice through the investment decision process. The book was inspired by the many questions he receives as assistant treasurer and plan administrator for The Times Mirror Company, where he is responsible for both the defined benefit and the 401(k) plans. Schwanbeck honed his communication skills as a former investor relations and communications professional.

401(k) Literature Summary, a quarterly journal, provides abstracts of current articles on 401(k) topics across a range of industry publications, including plan administration, investing, regulation and communications. Available from the 401(k) Company: 512-499-1700.

Money magazine's newsletter, *Retire with Money,* which it publishes specifically for organizations, is another useful source for educating plan participants.

Smart Money, and "Invest for Retirement" in particular, by James B. Stewart, which appeared in its November 1993 issue. This article helps the individual separate expectation from reality and integrate the many variables that enter into retirement planning, including assessing how priorities and goals change at different stages of life, what kind of retirement lifestyle is desired, and so on. It includes several helpful checklists.

Some plan sponsors encourage their employees to do their homework ("401(k) investing is a lot like buying a used car; you don't buy the first one you see"), and suggest they read the business section of local and national newspapers. *USA Today* produces consumer-oriented and easy-to-understand coverage of 401(k) investing, as does *The Wall Street Journal.*

"On the Risk of Stocks in the Long Run," by Zvie Bodie, *Financial Analysts Journal,* May/June 1995, pp. 18-22. Bodie, a professor of finance at Boston University, turns a sobering twist on the rule of thumb that claims stocks are the best investment over the long-term. Drawing on earlier, more technical arguments by economists Paul Samuelson and Robert Merton, Bodie uses the analogy of shortfall insurance (options as protection on a portfolio) to show that a long-term horizon won't necessarily mitigate short-term riskiness. The idea that stocks will always outperform if you can afford to hold through a downturn may be true, but what if that downturn lasts as long as your pre-retirement years—or retirement? Probability, he argues, is not in itself a measure of risk; severity matters, too. The percentage an investor allocates to stocks must relate to the individual's life and his exposure to other risks—and the potential impact of those risks.

"Participant Education Pays," by Lynn Brenner, *Plan Sponsor,* May 1995, pp. 20-26, discusses the innovative techniques sponsors are using to boost participation and attract hard-to-reach audiences.

Noteworthy industry resources include:
The Employee Benefit Research Institute publishes many useful research and special reports, books and public opinion surveys for the benefits community, all of unimpeachable quality. EBRI has produced a number of issue briefs on trends in 401(k) investing: its April 1995 *Can We Save Enough to Retire? Participant Education in Defined Contribution Plans* is the first of three devoted to education and 401(k)s. A forthcoming issue brief will present detailed tabulations of participant behavior in a few large pension plans and will evaluate the impact of various educational programs on participation rates, contribution levels and asset allocation. For subscription or membership information, call EBRI: 202-659-0670.

The Institute of Management & Administration (IOMA) an independent publisher of newsletters and reports for the defined contribution market (chiefly mid-sized and small plans), publishes *IOMA Performance Report.* IOMARate, its new fund ranking system, incorporates risk measures, covers non-public funds, in addition to listed mutual funds. Call (212) 244-0360.

SUGGESTIONS FROM THE UNDERWRITERS

CIGNA Retirement & Investment Services recommends:

"A Risk Roundtable," moderated by Claire Makin and Harvey D. Shapiro, *Institutional Investor,* September, 1995, p. 93. Six top investment professionals discuss how to define and control risk and the implications risk has for companies in the money management business.

MetLife suggests:

"Getting Back to the Basics," by Ronald D. Hurt, *Business Insurance,* April 3, 1995. Hurt, national director of employee communications for MetLife's defined contribution group, argues that plan sponsors should not let technology drive their plan's communication strategy. He outlines five basic steps for sponsors: decide on goals (if there are conflicting goals within management, negotiate down to one or two key objectives); discover your audience and the differences among employees by talking to them and actively soliciting feedback; develop a strategy and stick to it; sell the plan (remember, these plans are competing for disposable income against all the powers of Madison Avenue) and measure results.

Strong Capital Management offers:

Investing At Work, an 18-page, full-color 401(k) primer in magazine format that presents savings, investment and risk concepts with eye-catching visuals and a breezy, straightforward narrative style.

"Top Ten Don'ts for 401(k) Participants," by Rochelle Lamm Wallach, President of Strong Advisory Services. This no-nonsense article captures the big mistakes plan participants make and provides a concise, thought-provoking checklist of pitfalls for 401(k) participants to avoid.

"How Adults Learn: Teaching Not Telling in 401(k) Communications," by Pamela Gordon and Mary Jane Kipp, principals of Gordon Kipp Associates. This article, authored for Strong by two experienced educators, introduces the theory of adult education and its applicability to designing and implementing effective employee communications.

ORGANIZATIONS AND ASSOCIATIONS

American Society of Training and Development, 1640 King Street, Box 1443, Alexandria, VA 22313-2043. Phone 703-683-8100.

Institute of Certified Financial Planners, 7600 East Eastman Avenue, Suite 301, Denver, CO 80231-4397, phone 303-751-7600, can provide information and referrals on financial planners throughout the country, many of whom offer education and seminar programs.

The Financial Literacy Center produces a series of colorful, easy-to-read and inexpensive brochures to help educate 401(k) participants, as well as *Loose Change*, a newsletter written under the direction of the Institute of Certified Financial Planners. Call (616) 343-0770 or (800) 334-4094.

The 401(k) Association, founded by Ted Benna, provides a hotline as well as information services for plan participants. These include its investment guide, *Planning for Tomorrow*, and *Legislative Update*, a quarterly newsletter. Call (215) 579-8830.

The Profit Sharing/401(k) Council of America (PSCA), a non-profit association of 1,200 companies and their two million employees, produces communications tools to aid plan sponsors and provides help with plan design, administration, investment and compliance. It publishes an *Annual Survey of Profit-Sharing and 401(k) Plans*. Call (312) 441-8550.

GLOSSARY OF INVESTMENT RISKS

Accumulation Risk: Also called savings risk or shortfall risk, it's the risk of not accumulating enough money for a comfortable or secure retirement. If only one type of risk needed to be communicated, plan sponsors, investment managers and consultants agree unanimously—this is it.

Company Stock Risk: A classic example of diversification risk, but one worthy of its own designation. In a well-diversified portfolio, ownership of company stock is not inherently a risk, but frequently 401(k) investors are heavily invested in their own company's stock because their company match comes in that form. Often, company stock is their only equity investment. Company stock risk is a double whammy: apart from diversification risk—the risk that comes with concentrating investment assets in any one investment—there is the risk of a 401(k) investor's salary being tied to the company's fate along with his or her retirement savings. Discussing company stock is problematic for plan sponsors, since it is not politically correct to publicly dissuade company stock investment even though current allocation levels are alarming.

Credibility Risk: Will employees maintain their trust in an employer who doesn't adequately and responsibly explain investment risk? The concern plan sponsors share about credibility risk drives their efforts to educate participants about sound, prudent investing, including all types of risk that play a part in planning for a secure and comfortable retirement.

Credit (Quality) Risk: Also known as default risk, this is the ability of a bond issuer to pay interest and principal on a timely basis, or the likelihood that the issuer will default on principal or interest payments. Credit risk is not a consideration with U.S. Treasury securities since they are backed by "the full faith and credit" of the U.S. government, but it is a consideration with sovereign issues (foreign government bonds) and corporate and municipal bonds. Holders of Orange County, California bonds (or of a mutual fund containing these issues) experienced credit risk firsthand, as did investors holding Mexican bonds in late 1994 or Chrysler's bonds just before the company's landmark government bailout. Credit risk affects not only the value of an issuer's bonds: if financial distress is the reason for a company's low credit rating from Standard & Poor's or Moody's, its stock will also decline in value. Investors who want the prospect of higher returns can mitigate credit risk through diversification.

Currency Risk: This is the risk that changes in foreign exchange rates will reduce the dollar value of overseas investments. Since 1971, when the U.S. dollar came off the gold standard, it has "floated" in value as do all foreign currencies relative to each other. When the German Deutschmark rises against the U.S. dollar, the dollar value of a portfolio of German stocks or bonds, or of a fund containing them, will drop proportionately. Currency risk is a key risk of international investments because it can neutralize higher returns.

Diversification Risk: The risk associated with putting all your investment eggs in one basket—or simply not spreading them among enough baskets. Allocating investments to each of the main asset classes doesn't necessarily protect against diversification risk; investors need to be properly diversified within each asset class.

Inflation Risk: The potential loss of an investment's value due to inflation, which decreases the purchasing power of a dollar. This is the big risk inherent in lower-yielding investments, such as bonds. With an inflation rate of 2%, a 4% money market return is worth only 2% in pre-tax purchasing power. After savings risk, inflation risk is considered the biggest risk to 401(k) investors.

Interest Rate Risk: The potential for fixed-income investments to decline in value as interest rates rise. When prevailing interest rates go up relative to the rates of bonds an investor currently holds, the principal value of the bonds in his or her portfolio falls. The newer bonds offer a higher rate of return and are, therefore, worth more. Interest rate risk is the key risk of fixed-income investments.

Investment Risk: Sometimes a synonym for market risk; also used more generally to mean any of a variety of risks related to investing—market, inflation or interest rate risk, and so on. Because the 401(k) is a retirement vehicle and the investor's time horizon is usually long-range, investment risk can be minimized through sound asset allocation (diversification).

Loan Risk: When participants borrow money from their 401(k), they undermine the potential accumulation of assets for their retirement. In many cases, they do not repay loans. However, even when loans are repaid, that money will generally earn less because it is paid back at a fixed-rate, rather than at the rate it would have been earning if it had remained in an equity investment, for example. Loan risk is a subset of accumulation or savings risk, but it deserves its own designation because it is neither the result of non-participation nor of under-contribution to the plan. Loan risk can also be viewed as opportunity risk.

Market Risk: That portion of a particular security's risk that is common to all securities in its general class; the risk inherent across a broad market, such as the bond market or the stock market, which cannot be eliminated through diversification; the chance that an entire financial market may decline. 401(k) investors

YOUR EMPLOYEES MAY HAVE A FEW QUESTIONS ABOUT THEIR 401(k) PLAN

WE HAVE MORE THAN 100 ANSWERS

A New Way to Educate Plan Participants

I t's not surprising that plan participants have lots of questions about their 401(k) plan—how it works; what they can expect to withdraw from it and when; how to make the most sensible investments for their specific needs; whether or not they should even enroll.

As evidence mounts that employees are not investing early enough, wisely enough or simply **enough**, plan sponsors and administrators have an increasingly urgent obligation to respond by giving their employees a solid basis for making sound decisions about their future.

That's why this new book from Investors Press is so important.

A New Way to Boost Plan Enrollment

Written specifically for plan participants and eligible enrollees, **Building Your Nest Egg With Your 401(k)** gives them the confidence and knowledge they need to manage their 401(k). Exhaustively researched by its distinguished author Lynn Brenner— personal finance columnist for *Newsday*, a Times Mirror publication with more than a million readers—**Nest Egg** draws on Brenner's extensive experience and the results of interviews with more than 100 large and mid-range plan sponsors and administrators. In concise, *easy to understand* language, this important new book answers more than a hundred of the most commonly asked employee questions about 401(k)s. These independent, objective responses will help your employees make more informed judgements about the value of enrolling early, the maximum amount they should save and which investment vehicles will best help them meet their specific needs and expectations. Throughout this handsome book's 160 pages of text and 4-color tables, charts and graphs illustrate and explain key aspects of saving and investing. *Easy to understand*, thorough and entirely relevant to participant's practical needs, **Building Your Nest Egg With Your 401(k)** is also an ideal way for plan sponsors to comply with 404(c) voluntary guidelines and provide the impartial, third-party information participants need as they plan for a secure retirement.

should distinguish between market risk and market noise: the intra-day or day-to-day swings of the stock or bond markets that can be caused by any number of technical reasons, but that have no long-term significance.

Opportunity Risk: See Loan Risk

Pre-payment Risk: A risk assumed by anyone who invests in mortgage-backed bonds (Ginnie Maes) or mortgage-backed bond funds or asset-backed securities of any kind. If interest rates fall, homeowners pay off their existing mortgages and refinance them at the lower rates; holders of the bonds backing those mortgages get their principal back much sooner than expected and must then reinvest it at the lower prevailing interest rate.

Reinvestment Risk: The risk that investors won't match the yield of existing investments when they reinvest stock dividends, bond coupons or principal. Reinvestment risk is muted by the effect of a having a portfolio of diversified securities with mixed maturities and dividend payment streams. Reinvestment risk is rarely addressed in 401(k) communication materials, though it can have a big impact on returns over time. Many participants, for example, view GICs as a "safer" alternative to ordinary bond funds because of their guaranteed rates, without recognizing the reinvestment risk they face at maturity.

Savings Risk: See Accumulation Risk.

Tax Risk: What taxes can do to retirement savings upon retirement is an issue of great importance. Although tax risk is not currently a high priority on the 401(k) education list, it will no doubt begin to attract greater attention as education programs proliferate. The argument for pre-tax deferral presumes that people will be in lower tax brackets upon retirement. This presumption depends on many variables, including the participant's total financial assets and what state and Federal tax levels will be when the participant retires. These factors are impossible to predict, although it is likely that tax laws will differ substantially twenty years from now. Employees should consult with a tax adviser in order to consider the total tax picture.

Volatility: How subject an investment is to fluctuations in value in a market environment; the range of gain and loss in a given investment. The 1-, 3- and 5-year performance of a mutual fund might be positive, but within those periods there may have been quarters with negative returns. Defining volatility as "the value going up and down" may not convey risk, however. It may be more accurate to say that the more an investment's value moves up and down, the greater the likelihood it will be down the day an investor wants to take money out of it.

AUTHORS' BIOGRAPHIES

LYNN BRENNER writes regularly about personal finance, employee benefits and other business issues for both general circulation and national business publications, including *Newsday, The New York Times, CFO, Treasury & Risk Management, Financial World, Plan Sponsor* and *Corporate Finance*. She has written three books: **Building Your Nest Egg With Your 401(k): A Guide to Help You Achieve Retirement Security** (Investors Press, 1995); **The Insurance Information Institute's Handbook for Reporters**, a primer for journalists covering the insurance industry and **How to Get Your Money's Worth in Home and Auto Insurance,** a consumer book cited by *Money* magazine as one of the four best finance books of 1990. Before working independently, Ms. Brenner was a senior staff writer at *The Journal of Commerce, Institutional Investor* and *American Banker* successively for more than a decade, during which time she covered the insurance, banking and mutual fund industries.

DREW W. DEMAKIS, Managing Director of Research at Rogers, Casey & Associates, Inc., is responsible for asset class coverage and manager evaluations. He leads the firm's research process and client delivery efforts, managing the research specialists and overseeing all client investment programs. He also contributes to the strategic planning and development of the firm's systems and technology initiatives. Mr. Demakis's expertise in these areas adds an important dimension to the firm's client review committee, which meets on a weekly basis to discuss specific clients and topical issues. Before becoming research director, Mr. Demakis was a senior consultant in the consulting group, with lead responsibility for quantitative approaches to structuring investment programs. Before joining RogersCasey in 1987, he was an analyst with Chemical Bank, Tokyo, where he was responsible for developing systems for loan portfolios. Mr. Demakis graduated with a B.A. in Economics from the University of Chicago and an M.B.A. in Finance from Washington University.

RUTH HUGHES-GUDEN is Managing Director of the Defined Contribution Services Group at Rogers, Casey & Associates, Inc. Her responsibilities as group head include strategic planning and managing client relationships; she is also a member of the firm's client review committee. Ms. Hughes-Guden has been involved in the design, implementation and monitoring of defined contribution programs since 1983 and her broad industry experience has led to a wide range of speaking engagements at industry conferences. Most recently, she has contributed to the design and analysis of the firm's annual defined contribution survey. Before joining RogersCasey in 1983, Ms. Hughes-Guden worked for two years at a venture capital firm where she was responsible for screening proposals for future funding. She holds a B.A. in Psychology from St. Michael's College in Vermont and an M.B.A. from the University of Connecticut.

OTHER INVESTORS PRESS BOOKS

THE CHANGING FACE OF PENSION MANAGEMENT:
*Rescripting the Role of Plan Sponsors, Trustees,
Money Managers and Consultants*

May 1994

A WING AND A PRAYER: *Defined Contribution Plans
and the Pursuit of 24 Karat Golden Years*

August 1994

FILLING THE VACUUM: *Alternative Investments for
Pension Plans, Endowments and Foundations*
October 1994

EMERGING MARKETS: *A Map for Global Investors*

December 1994

HELPING EMPLOYEES ACHIEVE RETIREMENT SECURITY
Featuring Answers to the Most Often Asked 401(k) Questions

June 1995

INNOVATION FOR THE MILLENNIUM:
Creative Solutions for Pension Management

July 1995

ALPHA—THE POSITIVE SIDE OF RISK:
Daring to Be Different

February 1996

($45.00 per copy)

Please allow two weeks for delivery and specify quantity
and titles you are ordering. Payment and mailing instructions
should be faxed to 203-868-9733, or mailed to:

Investors Press Inc.
P.O. Box 329, Washington Depot, CT 06794